Making Your Phone Ring
with Internet Marketing
for Roofing Companies

Making Your Phone Ring
with Internet Marketing
for Roofing Companies

Welton Hong

Founder of Ring Ring Marketing [R]

www.RingRingMarketing.com

Printed in the United States of America

ISBN 978-0-9891830-3-1

Thanks to my parents Shunhua and Sumei for their guidance, my wife Ihsuan for just about everything, and to my siblings William and Jennifer who make it all worthwhile.

CONTENTS

INTRODUCTION:
The Yellow Pages is Dead; now Internet Marketing *IS* Marketing

Yes, it's true.

The Yellow Pages is dead.

(You'll note that I said the Yellow Pages *is* dead, as opposed to the Yellow Pages *are* dead. Yes, I know it sounds weird. Blame whoever gave a plural name to a singular directory.)

Don't feel guilty if you didn't get the news right away, or if you didn't send flowers or a card. The Yellow Pages died a peaceful death in its sleep. As a matter of fact, it's been sleeping for a long, long time.

The ultimate cause of death:

Irrelevancy.

Hang on, you say. The Yellow Pages isn't dead! I still get that thick book — maybe more than one — landing on my doorstep every six months or so.

Sure, it's not looking quite as vibrant as it once was — it's thinner, it's smaller, it's missing, well, a whole lot of stuff that used to be in it — but it's not dead.

Friend, do not fool yourself.

The Yellow Pages is dead. It just doesn't know it yet.

Remember the old Yellow Pages catchphrase? "Let your fingers do the walking."

Well, there you go. You can now call them The Walking Dead.

Here's what we mean:

Yes, some businesses still pay for listings in the Yellow Pages. Some businesses still pay for advertisements in the Yellow Pages. Your business might very well do *both*.

And for more than 100 years — the first "yellow pages" type of phone directory began in the 1880s — that made perfect sense.

In fact, if you wanted your business to be found by potential customers, you *had* to be in the Yellow Pages. To *not* be listed was business suicide. Most businesses needed to be listed *and* run an advertisement to compete in their local industries.

But then everything changed.

I'll return to that point in a second, but first: You're reading this book because you run a business that specializes in roof replacement and repair. That's exactly the type of business that traditionally has relied on print advertising, particularly in the Yellow Pages, to attract customers.

So I know that outright saying "the Yellow Pages is dead" might come as a shock. Depending on how long you've been in business, it probably performed very well for you for some time. And that's fine. Go ahead and take a moment to appreciate all it did for you in the past.

But the past is the past, and I pride myself in being completely honest with every one of my clients. If I told them they could still rely on print advertising as rocket forward into this digital age, that wouldn't be the truth.

I run a pay-for-results business. That means that if my client doesn't make money, I don't make money. I provide a 100 percent money-back guarantee for a full 60 days, so my business depends on the companies I work with making money — and fast.

So I can't afford to beat around the bush. I specialize in working with roofing companies and other home improvement businesses, and I've seen just how quickly their revenues grow when they expand from print advertising to the online world.

Change can be scary, but it can't be ignored.

The change was on the horizon when personal computers became standard in people's homes. But the big turn, the first one, occurred when a 24-7 Internet connection became more common than not.

That's when people realized they could just as easily jump on their computers and look up listings for local businesses without breaking out the phone book. And as more and more businesses invested in websites and listings on Google, Yahoo, Bing and similar sites, specific information about those businesses became available.

Businesses could provide far more information (at no extra cost) on their sites and listings than they ever could in a Yellow Pages listing or ad. Customer reviews, hours of business, recent testimonials — all of that and more was available to potential customers whenever they liked.

That was the status quo for a while, but another big sea change occurred over just the past couple of years with two great technological innovations: smartphones and tablets.

It's one thing to be able to access information from around the world in the comfort of your home. It's something else entirely to have that information available in the palm of your hand, 24 hours a day, no matter where you are: at the coffee shop, in the park, in your car.

As we head into 2014, smartphones are now far more powerful than a top-of-the-line personal computer was just a couple of years ago. The same is true of tablets. And with increases in speed and download power, it's now incredibly easy for someone with only the most basic understanding of technology to access all this information in seconds.

Businesses just like yours have taken advantage of this by optimizing their websites and listings for mobile technology. A couple of years ago, many of the websites you pulled up on your phone would be hard to read or even unintelligible, because those sites had been created to be viewed on a large computer monitor.

That's no longer the case. The most successful sites now appear in mobile versions that look perfectly fine on everything from a tablet to even a small smartphone. Businesses now create their own apps for smartphones, each specially designed to allow the user a broad variety of functions. A business that specializes in roof replacement and repair can showcase its services on a site that will look great on a desktop computer and still deliver an excellent visitor experience on a smaller screen.

The key to this transition: No longer are only the young or the especially tech-savvy looking for product or service information on their phones or tablets. Now, *everyone*, from a preteen to a great-grandmother, can do this quickly and easily. That's how far the technology has improved in a short time.

That's why the Yellow Pages are as good as extinct now, and types of print advertising from newspaper ads to magazines are continuing to plummet in reach and effectiveness.

These days, the term "marketing" means "Internet marketing." If you're not marketing your business on the Internet in today's world, you're virtually invisible to potential customers.

This is just as true for traditional brick-and-mortar businesses such as yours as it is for companies that do most (or all) of their business online.

As the owner of a roofing company, you have a number of potential marketing outlets available to you, but in today's digital age, one thing is irrefutable: If you're not promoting yourself online — and that doesn't just mean having a website you hope someone will happen across — you're fading from sight with every month that passes.

A recent survey showed that 90 percent of respondents felt that advertising in the Yellow Pages was ineffective. Only 3 percent of respondents said they used the Yellow Pages regularly, while *67 percent said they never use the Yellow Pages*. Can you afford to focus your marketing efforts in a directory that *2 out of 3 people never use*?

A recent survey showed that 90 percent of respondents felt that advertising in the Yellow Pages was ineffective.

Potential customers no longer necessarily call a friend when they're looking for a recommendation. Most go straight to Google (or Yahoo, or Bing) and do a search. It's free and convenient — the Internet is at our fingertips 24 hours a day — so why not?

You can think of the evolution from print marketing to Internet marketing as having a store that for many years was situated along a major road through your town. (It's true that for the roofing business, it's less common to have a brick-and-mortar shop that gets regular traffic from passersby, but play along with the metaphor for our purposes here.)

Let's say that for many years, people saw your shop by walking or driving by. Your building is there, your sign is there, and you're convenient to access.

Let's extend the hypothetical situation: A major U.S. highway is built in your town, just a few blocks from your store. Suddenly all the traffic comes down that highway, not the (once-) major road where your store still resides. No one travels down your road anymore.

You can have a great store, but no one knows you're there. You might even be better than the stores now situated along the U.S. highway, but they're the stores people see. They're convenient to access. Those stores are *where the people are*.

Today, the Internet is where the people are. And you get their attention by having a website that's optimized to be found when people are looking for what you do, specifically in your local market. You get their attention by having comprehensive business listings on Google and other major Internet sites. You get their attention by promoting your business on Facebook, Twitter, Pinterest and other social media sites. (And, as time changes, on other social media sites as they become popular — in today's world, nothing is ever static. It's ever-changing, and you need to be prepared to roll with the changes.)

That might all sound like a lot, but it really isn't. If you need a hand with the technical issues, qualified Internet marketing experts can handle those matters, letting you focus on what you do well: replacing and repairing roofs.

The key is to understand that online marketing is no longer just a single facet of your marketing plan. *It is the foundation of your marketing plan.* Business owners who ignore this fact will find themselves being ignored as we continue into this digital age.

It doesn't matter how traditional or blue-collar your customers are; everyone from farmers to housewives (or, for that matter, house husbands) now find local businesses through the Internet. If you're not promoting yourself there — and that means *actively* promoting yourself there — you don't exist.

In the rest of this book, I'll go over the basics of how Internet marketing works. I'll explain how an online marketing professional can help you attract massive quantities of new customers and ensure that you retain the ones you currently have.

I'll show you how a range of tools — many of them quite simple and affordable — can expand the reach of your company exponentially, regardless of whether you do business locally, statewide, nationwide or around the world.

No matter what, the key thing I hope you'll understand is that every month that goes by — heck, every week that goes by — without actively promoting your roofing company online is a massive waste of potential. The playing field keeps changing all the time, and it's incredibly easy to get left behind.

The good news is this: If you act soon and get your "online house" in order, you won't just be benefitting from everything that a well-designed Internet marketing campaign can do for you. You'll also have a massive advantage on local competitors in the roofing industry who have been slow to adapt to the new online marketing world.

You'll be recording in digital while they're still recording in analog. You'll be transmitting in high-definition while they're still using rabbit ears. You'll be operating in the present while they're still operating in the past. And that's a *gigantic* advantage in today's business world.

You want to be the roofing business holding that advantage, not the one watching from the sidelines. From this point forward, Internet marketing *is* marketing, and I'm here to show you how to take advantage.

Section 1:

Lead Generation

CHAPTER 1
Search Engine Marketing (SEM)

If your roofing business has a website, it's a fair bet you have at least some idea of what search engine marketing (SEM) entails.

(If your business doesn't have a website, that's a problem that really needs to be rectified *immediately*. Having a website is a bare minimum requirement for a business in the 21st century, and it has been for some time.

Without one, you might as well not have a front door or a phone. It's absolutely integral.

Regardless, let's go over the basics of what SEM is. In a nutshell, it's an umbrella term for a variety of tools that provide your site the best possible visibility given certain factors.

In other words, you're obviously not necessarily competing for visibility against every other site in the world. No matter what you do, you're not going to be more visible than Amazon for retail goods or more visible than iTunes more music sales.

In SEM, you want your site to be more visible than the sites of your natural competitors. As a local business, that means optimizing your site (and your marketing efforts) to rank higher in search engine results pages (SERPs) than other roofing companies in your market and in the area you serve.

These days, online search is extremely specialized. There are strategies and tools that let you put your best foot forward in a particular area and market.

Some of these tools require no advertising dollars; by optimizing your site with particular keywords and types of content, the site will organically rank well in your market and area.

Other tools require dipping into your marketing budget, such as allowing you to bid on particular keywords that people who are looking for your type of service will be using when they search.

For your business, this likely would include various forms of keyword phrases such as *roofer, roofing, roofing contractor, roofing service, roof installation, roof repair, roof replacement, roof repair, roofing repair, roofing company*, and so on, in addition to geographic keywords specific to the location upon ns which your business focuses. (This is just a small sample of possible keyword phrases to use.)

A successful Internet marketing plan typically combines both approaches, one that balances the initiatives of organic SEO and paid advertising.

In this chapter, I'll cover the basics of pay-per-click advertising (PPC), local search optimization, and Search Engine Optimization (SEO).

Pay-Per-Click Advertising (PPC)

Pay-per-click (PPC) is an umbrella term for several types of advertising, such as sponsored listings, paid search, partner ads, or sponsored links — with one thing in common: In each type, you pay for the ad only when a user clicks it and is forwarded to your website (or whatever destination page you set up).

Most often, you'll find PPC ads along the borders of the pages when you do online searches — you'll recall those pages are called SERPs, or search engine results pages. While Google remains the industry leader in search, Bing and Yahoo also get heavy usage as late 2013, and all three sites' SERPs are primary destinations for PPC ads.

One of the coolest things about PPC ads is that they don't appear until someone completes a search. Because they're dynamic, the ads that do appear following the search will be relevant to whatever the user is searching for. The ads are by definition targeting an interested party.

The other obvious benefit is that the ad doesn't cost you a penny simply for appearing — you only pay when it gets clicked, sending the user to your page and providing an opportunity to convert the visitor into a customer.

Creating a PPC account can differ slightly depending on the platform (typically Google, Yahoo, or Bing, though there are others), and an Internet marketing professional can explain the process and handle it for you. But here's the general game plan:

First, you'll create a PPC account with the particular platform, a simple enough process. Next, you'll create campaigns and ad groups.

The campaign part is where you determine options such as the geography of the market you wish to reach. Because you have a local business that relies on local customers, for example, you'll obviously want to target — that's right — local people.

(That's how localized search and advertising is these days: You can set it up so only people in your city, county, or state, for the most part, see your ads and thus click on them. However, if you also happen to do roofing work statewide or even nationwide — or partner with businesses that do — those options can be included as well.)

The ad groups comprise your advertisements and keyword lists. An Internet marketing professional can help you determine which terms people will be searching for when they want to find a residential or commercial roofing business (depending on which service you provide, or both).

Remember that despite the name, a keyword isn't necessarily just a single word; it's very often a phrase. You'll incorporate these keywords in the ads you run in your campaign.

The particular search engine for that campaign will determine how well the advertiser's campaigns and keywords match the user's particular search, and it will display the ads if there's a close match.

There are a few other factors that determine whether your ad will show up. Every search engine has an algorithm that considers these factors and employs them with each search. These factors include:

- How closely do the keywords in the list match the actual search?
- Does the advertisement itself include a mention of what the user is looking for?
- Does the ad forward the user to a landing page that is selling the product or service the user wants?
- How much are you willing to pay for a user searching for these terms to see your ad (and hopefully click through to it)?

The final point, the actual amount of your bid, determines not only how much you'll pay, but also how prominently your ad is displayed on the page.

The specifics of each search engine's algorithm are not made public for a sound reason: It keeps less legitimate advertisers from gaming the system, crafting ads that exist only to get clicks without actually providing the user anything useful.

Google, in particular, has been tweaking its algorithms substantially in recent years to reward websites and advertisers who are legitimately providing good information and selling useful services and products. This is happening not only in PPC but in search engine rankings; we'll talk about this some more later.

The thing to remember is this: If you provide good content on your website/landing page and craft good PPC ads to market your business, you'll be rewarded.

If your sites and ads are intended to mislead people into clicking through just to increase site traffic, you're taking a chance on being penalized by search providers, particularly Google.

A legitimate, reputable Internet marketing firm won't design a campaign like that (known as "black hat" in the industry) for you, because whatever short-term benefits a business might receive will be far outweighed by the massive damage it can do when Google sniffs it out. And Google will sniff it out: It's like the IRS — just much faster and smarter.

Whether PPC is a valuable investment for your business depends on several considerations. A big one is whether your website/landing page typically shows up near the top of the results when people are search-ing for the types of products and services you provide in your area.

As anyone can tell you, many people don't bother searching past the first page of SERPs. (Think about it: How often do you continue to Page 2 or 3 after doing a Google search?)

Being ranked on that first page is critical. If you're not ranked for whatever reason — perhaps your site isn't sufficiently optimized for search engines, or you're in a highly competitive market — you're virtually in-visible even if you're near the top of the listings on Page 2. If you're even deeper in the SERPs, you're in much bigger trouble. Most searchers, if they don't find what they're looking for by Page 2, will just try a new search with some different keywords.

A PPC ad lets you essentially jump ahead of the SERP organic listings, putting your site/landing page right out front. Granted, this comes at a price, and some searchers can be reluctant to click on an ad as opposed to a search result per se.

However, PPC remains a very effective tool for many reasons. It provides a lot of control and is highly customizable. You only pay if the ad is clicked. It also makes it easy to get accurate statistics on whether your ad is effective, unlike traditional types of advertising.

The analytics of PPC ads allows you to know which keywords people used to find your page, so you can tweak your keywords depending on which worked well (or poorly). You'll know how many people departed your page immediately after reaching it — and how many stuck around.

One of the biggest benefits of PPC (aka paid search) advertising is that it bridges the time gap between SEO improvements to your website and when they're recognized by Google.

Improving your organic SEO (the right way) goes a long way toward elevating your search rankings for people searching for roofing businesses in your area. However, Google only "crawls" your site (more on that later) occasionally, so it won't know immediately that you should be ranked high on the first page of results.

By comparison, PPC ads post almost immediately, letting you get your name right out front while you're waiting on Google to review your site and increase your organic ranking.

Some other benefits to PPC advertising to hone in on the right demographics and target the best leads:

Geography: This is a key factor in ensuring that you're targeting the most qualified leads. Analytical information allows you to tweak the geography of your ads to concentrate on markets where they're doing well (and perhaps pull them from markets where you're not garnering interest).

Similarly, one of the most useful aspects of PPC advertising is that you can target potential customers in very specific geographic areas.

For example, a PPC ad can be set to only appear within a set radius of a business's physical location. This is an *excellent* option for roofers, because anyone who needs roof repair and replacement obviously wants a local provider who can do installations quickly and conveniently. No one's in the market for an out-of-town roofer, at least not one who's *way* out of town.

In addition to radius, PPC ads can be set to run only in particular ZIP codes or cities. Whatever exact areas you wish to target, your PPC ads can be focused entirely on them.

If you want to cast a broader net, no problem. Unlike physical media such as the Yellow Pages, it costs *nothing extra* to target multiple cities. You're not paying five or six times as much to run an ad in five or six cities — it is one price fits all. Thus the cost per lead is far less expensive than it would be with traditional media.

Day parting: As with geographical targeting, PPC ads can be set up to run only during the times of the day or week you want them to run. If your roofing business is only open Monday through Friday, you might want your ads running only on those days.

If you mostly do commercial work, and thus your roofing clients are generally other local businesses, you can set your ads to run Monday through Friday from 9 to 5. Or, if you believe your potential customers are most likely to see your ads on weekends or at night, you can set them for those time frames.

Day	Time period	Midnight	4:00 AM	8:00 AM	Noon	4:00 PM	8:00 PM
Monday	07:00 AM - 07:00 PM						
Tuesday	07:00 AM - 05:00 PM						
Wednesday	Running all day						
Thursday	Running all day						
Friday	Noon - 04:00 PM						
Saturday	Running all day						
Sunday	Running all day						

Controlling lead flow: The scheduling of PPC ads can be easily modified to increase traffic. Google charges based on a daily budget.

Let's say you typically spend $20 per day, but there's a stretch where you need more business and have some budget flexibility. You can increase it to $30 for more coverage and thus more leads.

On the other hand, let's say you're already swimming in clients. You knock it down to $10 for a while to save some money and ensure you don't get overwhelmed. If you're too busy already, why spend money on ads?

You can even pause your ads for whatever time frame you determine if you go on vacation, are remodeling, etc. In this sense, running PPC ads is like turning the knob on a faucet: You can open it up to flow freely, turn it down to a trickle, or turn it off entirely for a while, all dependent on your needs at the time.

Seasonal businesses: This flexibility also is great for companies who do most of their business in particular seasons or want to advertise different services during a particular season. Your business likely has slow periods and busy periods, especially if — as in most places — the weather you are changes drastically from, say, June to February. If you tend to run promotions during slow periods, you can schedule those promotions to run throughout the slow season and immediately switch off when your business naturally picks up. Because roofs are commonly inspected in spring and fall, these are naturally prime periods to target homeowners who are determining they might your services.

Instant traffic: As I noted before, PPC ads allow you to be seen on the first page of search results almost immediately. You're paying for the opportunity to jump to the front of the pack.

This makes PPC a powerful tool for seeing a very fast return on an Internet marketing campaign. When used in tandem with organic SEO and local optimization strategies, you can see your traffic, qualified leads and conversions soar and continue climbing in both the short and long term.

PPC ads are never static: Anything can be tweaked, adjusted, or swapped out at any time. With traditional media such as the Yellow Pages, you're stuck with the same print ad for the entire year. You could start specializing in something entirely different, add a second (or third, or fourth) store, change your phone number or operating hours — and the Yellow Pages ad will still have all the old information until it's time for a new directory.

PPC ads let you change the content on the fly. If you want to run a promotion or a coupon, you can have it in front of potential customers in a matter of days.

Trying lots of variations: With a typical print ad, you come up with terms and phrasing you think will work best, cross your fingers, and hope it does the job.

PPC advertising allows you to try out many different variations of ads catered to the keywords you want. You can have hundreds of different variations employed at the same time. This also allows for **split testing** of the different choices, letting you know quickly which ads have the most impact and which are less successful.

Additionally, when you have several ads running simultaneously with differently worded keyword phrases, the ads people see will typically match up with the terms they're specifically searching for. If they search for "roof repair," they'll get the ad with that focus. If they search for "roof replacement," they'll get the ad with *that* focus.

This is another way in which PPC advertising beats out print, because in something such as the Yellow Pages, you simply have to determine which sections you want to be listed in and place ads in all of them.

Excellent branding tool: If improving brand awareness of your company or product is a critical concern, PPC is an effective tool to use. If people click on your ad, great: You're getting leads to come to your website. If they don't, you're still getting exposure to lots of people searching for the sort of thing you offer, improving your brand awareness.

You don't necessarily have to pay for the top spot: Consider the NFL draft. Teams regularly trade down from their initial spots in the draft because the value isn't there for the player they need in a particular position.

They can get that player even when they pick a little further down in the draft — and ultimately pay less money for the player, because the spot where a player is picked goes a long way toward determining his salary. (In the draft, teams can also get more draft picks for trading away a high pick, but that part's less relevant here.)

The same is true of PPC advertising. For most industries, typically including roofing, bidding for the top spot costs a lot more than the value it delivers. The top spot for a particular keyword is much more expensive than, let's say, the fourth spot.

Having that top spot makes sense for a business for which people will likely not take the time to perform any additional research — for example, a locksmith or a bail bonds provider. People often click on the very first ad that pops up when it's an emergency or time is of the essence.

However, as with your business, if a potential customer is going to be investing substantial money into a replacement roof — not to mention investing in an asset as valuable as one's house — that person isn't going to simply click on the first ad. That person will be checking out *several* advertisers that pop up for those keywords. In this situation, ranking third or fourth is *just as good as ranking first*, and it's markedly less expensive.

Additionally, when you're ranked somewhere between fourth and sixth, you're likely getting a better lead. These are people who take the time to research several options. They're clearly highly motivated to purchase your product and/or service, because otherwise they wouldn't be doing such extensive research.

PPC also can include display ads: While the focus of this discussion has been PPC ads that appear on search engine results pages, you can also do display ads on the pages of Google's display ad partners. These are the types of ads you see on larger websites.

In general, advertising for SERPs is intended for to attract customers who are ready to buy immediately. Display ads on larger websites are intended for branding and to attract customers who might be interested in your products or services at some time.

This is technically referred to as the Google Display Network. Google has introduced what it calls "flexible reach" targeting, which allows for greater control over targeting and the ability to try out different targeting combinations more easily.

Remarketing: This is another great benefit of PPC advertising. When you do Google PPC ads, you can elect to do remarketing, which means that your ads will continue to make a case for your business with people who have shown an interest in your products or services by visiting your site previously.

Google can track who has visited your site and continue to display your ads for these leads when they visit other sites. This allows you to reengage with leads who did not purchase immediately. You can even customize the messaging in this ad to make a special offer that will compel them to return to your site and do business with you.

Summary of PPC advantages

Virtually instant traffic to your advertisements
- You can have ads on the front pages of Google, Bing, and Yahoo in just few hours

A world of options print Yellow Pages can't provide
- Use text-based ads, streaming video ads, banner ads, and more

- Advertise to a targeted audience in minutes
- Be rewarded for creating good ads with lower ad costs

Laser targeting
- Advertise to people who are looking right now for what you're offering
- Quickly test to determine which ads bring you qualified traffic
- Easily monitor which keywords bring visitors who actually convert into customers and which do not, allowing you to easily alter your ad to include the highest-converting keywords

Local/regional targeting
- Target users by location, allowing you to specifically reach local customers
- Reach a worldwide audience, target your local area, or do both
- You can choose where and when you want your ads to be visible

Cost-effectiveness
- Pay only when a customer clicks on your ad
- Benefit from free branding even when people don't click on your ad
- Determine your costs based on your own objectives — specify exactly how much you want to spend, and even set a maximum daily and/or monthly budget

Powerful money-making tool

- If you could spend one dollar to make two dollars, how many dollars would you spend? That's exactly how a well-optimized PPC campaign works.

Measurable Results

- Real-time return-on-investment data using conversion tracking data
- Every aspect of the process is trackable
- Google collects and analyzes all key data for you and will auto-send you reports

Summary of PPC disadvantages

- Only through paying the advertising cost will you be able to determine the return on investment (ROI) of various ads.
- Every new visitor costs money: While you could get some return visitors who bookmark your site, in general when you stop paying, the visitors stop coming.
- Having your ads link to a high-converting site is a must: A good PPC campaign can drive lots of targeted traffic to your site, but if that site doesn't turn visitors into customers, it's wasted money.

A note on the landing page

With all that said, a PPC ad campaign is only as good as the landing page it's selling.

Let's say you're looking for a home and you drive past a gorgeous billboard advertising an amazing condominium complex just a mile away. It's advertising resort living at a fraction of the price, tons of amenities, and a great neighborhood.

So you head over to the address and discover... it's a dump. It looks like it hasn't been renovated in 100 years, it has a rusty, broken gate out front, and the parking lot is covered in trash that's clearly been piling up for weeks. (And let's say the roof is a wreck as well, because the owners haven't contracted with your great business to fix it.)

Are you going to bother driving in and checking it out? Or are you going to get the hell out of there before you get mugged?

That's what happens when a landing page doesn't deliver what the PPC ad promised. If the landing page is poorly designed, or if the website isn't selling what the typical visitor would expect, the visitor is going to "click out" in a matter of seconds. And you just paid for a visit that did you no good.

I'll get into landing page and website optimization more in a bit, but it's critical to remember that there's no point to doing PPC ads if you're sending visitors somewhere they don't want to be. Anything from a lack of relevant content to slow page loads can prompt a visitor to set sail in a matter of seconds.

Local Search Optimization

In the most basic sense, when we're talking about local search — sometimes also capitalized as Local Search — we're simply referring to online searches that have a geographical component.

If you live in St. Petersburg, Florida, and you need to have a replacement odometer installed (by a trained mechanic) for your 2005 Volkswagen Jetta, you're not going to want to simply search 2005 Volkswagen Jetta odometer or Volkswagen Jetta mechanic or 2005 Volkswagen Jetta repair.

You're going to want something that includes your actual location. So you'll add St. Petersburg to your search terms. If you're searching in English, you'll far more likely get results for Florida's St. Petersburg than the Russian city, but depending on what the results are, you might need to add Florida.

Of course, St. Petersburg is also part of the Tampa Bay metropolitan area, with both Tampa and Clearwater each just a short drive away. So you might want to expand your search to Tampa Bay or to each of those particular cities.

In recent years, search has become increasingly local. Again, this owes a lot to the massive expansion of affordable mobile technology. Smartphones and tablets allow people to navigate their neighborhoods easily with the help of the Internet.

According to Google, a full 20 percent of Web searches done now are local. When you limit that to only mobile searches (on a smartphone or tablet), that number *doubles to 40 percent*. Google also notes that 97 percent of Google users search online for local businesses at some point.

It's actually rather ironic: In its early days, the Internet allowed us to quickly and easily interact with people and places all around the world. These days, we're more likely to use it to find places and services right in our hometowns.

Of course, that's why local search optimization is so critical for local roofing companies in 2013 and beyond. As I noted in the introduction, this is how people find your company these days. They don't bother opening up the Yellow Pages (if they even have that book lying around the house, which is unlikely). They search on their PC, or tablet, or smartphone.

Optimizing your business for local search ensures not only that you're putting your best foot forward for potential local customers — it ensures that you show up at all. You need to do this to show up on Google Maps, the most widely used graphical search provider in the world.

Practically every day, I find myself needing to know where something is near my location — an ATM, a gas station, a restaurant, a grocery store. My phone automatically knows where I am, thanks to GPS. Businesses that are optimized for local search will pop up as soon as I search, and the listings show me how far away they are, directions, etc.

But that's not all: When a business has included its business hours on its Google+ Local listing, I automatically know whether it's open or closed — or how long I have to get there until it *does* close.

I can also see ratings and reviews from customers, helping me know whether I can trust that particular mechanic, hair stylist, or retailer.

As I noted before, this is one of the key processes people now use to find local businesses. If you're not taking advantage of it — if your business isn't listed in Google or Bing, or if the information there is out of date or incomplete — you're placing yourself at a massive disadvantage compared to your competitors.

Getting to know Google+ Local

Your first thought might well be that Google+ Local is an extraordinarily silly name for what is now one of the most important marketing tools for local businesses.

And you're right.

Google likes silly names for its services. It also likes changing names, so maybe you won't be stuck with it for too long.

Google is really amazing at all sorts of things, but it also never met anything it didn't want to tweak, rename, tweak again, rename again, discontinue, and then revive with another name. Hey, that's just Google.

But don't be scared away from Google+ Local just because it has a silly name. (It used to be Google Places, a name that made so much sense it obviously had to go.) It's a product of Google's wanting to merge its

Google+ (aka Google Plus) social media platform with its Google Local listings platform.

Google+ (the social media aspect itself) hasn't exactly been a big hit for the worldwide leader in search, so it's been adding the "plus" to all sorts of things. And it actually makes some degree of sense in this case, because social media functionality is now part of how Google does its local search.

But let's bang out the basics of Google+ Local. Google itself says the service "helps users discover and share places," which puts the two-headed snake in context in a mere six words: *discover*, which is the foundation of local search, and *share*, which is the foundation of social media.

It's a tool intended to get potential customers not only finding your business, but also sharing the word with others. Which is a mighty powerful thing when it's backed by the power (and money — lots and lots and lots of money) of Google.

When a potential customer does a Google search, accesses Google Maps, or uses a growing number of other Google services, Google+ Local will provide that person place recommendations based on several criteria.

Those include the person's location, reviews that person has written of other places on Google, and even the person's "circles" — if you haven't used Google+, those are roughly equivalent to "Likes" on Facebook.

Google+ users can add people, places, and interests to their Google circles, allowing them to categorize those entities in various circles based on topics, interests, or really whatever. The circles are basically subsets of their entire set of connections.

With Google+ Local, users can publish reviews and photographs of places they visit. They can view a Zagat summary — a rating based on the well-known Zagat system — of other users' reviews.

They can visit the business's local Google+ page, and if the page has been properly filled out by the business's owner or webmaster — many still are not — the searcher can find location information, operating hours, phone number(s), a map, average prices, etc.

Google+ Local results aren't limited to people searching in Google+. They will pop up in search results anytime a user does a search with local intent (something that includes a geographic term, generally). These local results most often are displayed at or near the top of the SERP, providing excellent visibility for local businesses.

However, having a fully realized Google+ Local page is even more beneficial when people search specifically in Google+. Those results will only show Google+ Local pages. Your page won't be competing for visibility with websites, the aforementioned PPC ads, or anything else that could distract the searcher.

Similarly, your business's appearance on Google Maps will include information from your Google+ Local listing, including information such as reviews, which can be powerful business drivers. As you know, people will want as much information as possible before choosing a provider to renovate an asset as important as their home — not to mention letting people *into* their home to do installation. Having the strongest reputation in your area immediately makes you a front-runner for these services.

Surveys show that 72 percent of consumers consider online reviews as trustworthy as personal recommendations, which is why ensuring you have positive (and preferably exceptionally positive) reviews on your Google+ Local listing is so important.

Make sure to ask happy customers to leave positive reviews on your listing, which will amp up your Zagat rating. Often people viewing map listings will notice the Zagat rating long before individual reviews, so it's a crucial consideration.

Your Google+ Local listing also effectively acts as a blog or Facebook page. You can provide updates and reach out to customers there, which not only provides useful information (on promotions, sales, special events, etc.) but shows potential customers you're highly engaged and communicative.

Don't forget Bing Local

Of course, Bing has its own local option, and while it makes sense to make Google+ Local your top priority, it would be a mistake to ignore Bing. It is the number-two search option for consumers, and being powered by Microsoft, it has a lot of muscle behind it.

There are, expectedly, a lot of similarities between the two listings services. Your roofing company no doubt has a physical address, so it likely already has a Bing Local listing, and you can claim it by using the Bing Business Portal.

Much as with Google+ Local, you'll want to ensure your profile is completed with all the pertinent information for your business.

Unlike Google+ Local, Bing Local doesn't have its own native reviews as of this writing. Instead, it's partnered with Yelp (as with Yahoo, we're going to leave off the exclamation point for simplicity), one of the most popular online review services.

However, other reviews from third-party services can appear on your Bing Local page, including reviews from Citysearch.

There are some other differences between these two platforms, and it's useful to note that Yahoo has a local platform of its own, but most of the points noted earlier about Google+ Local relate to all the services.

The most important takeaway is that completing all your business's information on these platforms — and ensuring it's accurate and kept up to date — is necessary for putting your best foot forward when people are searching for local businesses. These services are built to accommodate mobile users, a base that's expanding rapidly every day.

Roofing Contractors near **San Jose, California** ⊘

bing.com/local

① Platinum Roofing Inc
1900 Dobbin Dr San Jose, CA 95133 · (408) 272-9595
Directions

★★★★★
6 reviews ›

② Economy Roofing Inc
2988 Neal Ave San Jose, CA 95128 · (408) 615-7200
Directions

★★★★★
1 review ›

③ Los Gatos Roofing · Bing Local
888 Faulstich Ct San Jose, CA 95112 · (408) 298-9399
Directions

★★★★★
33 reviews ›

④ Lindy Roofing Co.
476 W Taylor St San Jose, CA 95110 · (408) 286-9990
Directions

★★★★★
15 reviews ›

⑤ Platinum Roofing Inc · Bing Local
2943 Daylight Way San Jose, CA 95111 · (408) 280-5028
Directions

Directions ›

Citations

Another important aspect of local search optimization is the use of citations. These are effectively mentions of your business that appear on the Internet regardless of whether there's an actual link to your website.

A citation — also known as a "Web reference" — could occur when your business is noted in general text in an online listing of companies in your local market or region. It could be a mention in a news story, white paper, or trend piece.

Even though these references to your business don't include a direct link, they are key components in the ranking algorithms of Google and the other top search engines.

The more you're referenced on other sites, especially if they're among the more regularly visited and indexed sites, the more "useful" the search engines think your business is. This improves the rankings of your business's website.

A citation on something such as a chamber of commerce or county business index is especially useful. This is also true of a citation in a major newspaper or other news site.

That's because these citations lend even more legitimacy and credibility to your site — it's awfully hard to "fake" an appearance in a major newspaper, so the search engine knows you're an actual operating business.

Your Internet marketing specialist can help you learn how to improve your citations, but in general, the key is to ensure you're properly listed in all legitimate listing services that are appropriate for your business.

Be sure you're included in local blogs, locally focused directories, and directories/blogs that are specific to your particular industry.

If you are involved with something newsworthy that can get your business named in a newspaper story or on a local television station's website — such as providing free or discounted roofing work for Habitat for Humanity or a similar housing-related charity — that's a great citation to have.

Quick tip: Doing community service such as this is a spectacular way to get publicity for a commercial business, because the local news rarely covers such businesses (excepting paid advertising) outside of brief listings, and news stories are the types of citations Google and other search engines will prioritize.

Local search advantages

- It's free, which allows for infinite return on investment
- Allows customers to rate and review your business, so if you're good at what you do, you'll stand out from the crowd
- Adds your site to Google Maps, one of the top ways people discover local businesses now
- Lets you add specific keywords to your business description, giving you a leg up on competitors who have not done this

Local search disadvantages

- Only seven businesses automatically show up as a search result
- It can take greater than a month to show up in the listings, and the likelihood of appearing high in the results (or in the first seven at all) depends on optimization
- You can only optimize your business for the five to ten most relevant keywords

Search Engine Optimization (SEO)

An entire book can be written about Search Engine Optimization (SEO). In fact, many have been, and many more will be. There are many facets to SEO, and best practices are regularly changing. Here, I'll touch on the highlights.

You undoubtedly know the purpose of SEO: It's a set of processes intended to help ensure your website/landing page ranks as highly as possible in search results.

Ever since search engines began appearing on the Internet, website owners and webmasters have understood the power of ranking as highly as possible on SERPs (which stands for search engine result pages, as you'll recall).

It's not exactly a new concept: Everything else being equal, you're more likely to get people's business if yours is the first option they see.

That's why print magazines (still around for now, but disappearing) want to be at the front of the racks in bookstores (also, sadly, disappearing).

That's why businesses for many years would select names that would put them at the front of white pages and Yellow Pages (you already know they're disappearing) listings: Ace Plumbing was upstaged by Abacus Plumbing, followed by Aardvark Plumbing, followed by A Aardvark Plumbing, followed by A AA Aardvark Plumbing… you know how it goes.

In the digital age, alphabetization doesn't matter (unless someone sorts a list alphabetically to find a particular link, that is). Search engines don't care whether you have a really colorful name or a bland one — that's not part of the equation.

Granted, your business's name *does* matter, but only in the sense that the SEO will be improved if terms in the name are highly relevant to what people will be searching for. That is, if you sell custom hubcaps in Des Moines, naming your business Des Moines Custom Hubcaps (and snagging that as a domain name as well) will be a big help for your SEO. If you're a roofer in Phoenix, obviously, something such as Phoenix Roofing (or Phoenix Roof Repair and Replacement, etc.) makes things easy for search engines and potential leads.

But before we dig into how SEO works, let's start off by defining a few terms:

White hat SEO vs. black hat SEO: I mentioned black hat SEO earlier, but here's a little more context.

As soon as webmasters realized that search engines were using certain elements of websites to determine how highly those sites should rank, some started to think of ways to game the system. When a site is using tricks that are only intended to improve rankings or traffic without providing an equivalent benefit to actual visitors, that's **black hat SEO**.

On the other hand, when a site uses techniques that improve rankings and traffic that are integral to providing a benefit for visitors, that's **white hat SEO**. Many sites benefited from black hat SEO for many years, but search engines (particularly Google) have tweaked their algorithms substantially in recent years to punish sites using black hat tactics and reward ones who follow a white hat approach.

As I noted earlier, it's simply not worth it to work with a firm that promises big results through black hat practices, no matter how cheap the price. The money you save up front by working with these con artists — because that's truly what they are — won't come close to making up for the business you lose when Google banishes your site to page eight of its SERPS. In extreme cases, Google can even *ban your URL altogether*. And once you're on Google's bad side, you're in trouble: Google has a very long memory.

Spiders/crawling: With rare exception, search engines don't employ people to actually visit websites and determine whether those sites are relevant and useful (and thus worthy of being ranked highly). They create software known as **spiders**. These spiders go to websites and then read and index the information there, a process known as **crawling** the site.

They don't just review the content visitors can see, but also information in the coding of the site. The info they collect is then factored into complicated algorithms that determine how highly a site should be ranked for various searches people do on the Web.

Organic search results: Otherwise known as **natural search results**, these are the basic unpaid search results — as opposed to paid listings, "sponsored" listings, or ads — people get when they search for keywords. As you've surely noticed, searching for anything on the major sites these days will result in a page of SERPs that include both organic and paid results, and sometimes it can be tricky to tell the difference.

Ultimately, your roofing company's website or landing page has two very distinct objectives.

One objective is to put your best foot forward for actual human visitors. You want people who visit your site to be impressed by your business and want to do work with you. (This is especially critical in your industry, where your clients are intelligent, responsible homeowners who will factor your trustworthiness highly into whether they want to contract with you.)

You want **conversions** — converting these visits into phone calls from new customers and actual sales. To this end, you want the content on your site to read well, provide useful information, and sell the visitor on the fact that you can get the job done.

The other objective is to sell the relevance of your site to the search engine spiders. This is where SEO strategies come into play. By employing these strategies in the site's content, design, and coding, you can persuade these spiders to rank your site highly when people search for keywords that would be naturally associated with your roofing business.

As you might expect, one of the greatest concerns Google and other search providers have is that sites try to game the system to make the *spiders* happy without making actual human *visitors* happy. This is why Google, in particular, has started heavily penalizing sites that use this approach. It wants the sites that rank highest to be the most useful for actual people who are actively searching for what you provide.

You might wonder why certain sites would game the system with pages that rank highly but provide nothing good for the visitors. People will just click out immediately when they realize there's nothing there for them, right?

Some site owners/webmasters do this because their business model simply pays them for **hits** — visits to sites, whether the visitors click out immediately or not. Many use advertising models where it doesn't matter whether the site itself is useful, just that they've recorded hits for advertisers to the site.

If someone goes on to click on an ad on the site, they get paid even more. Essentially, they're not really selling anything or providing any service; they exist only to trick people, essentially, into clicking through to the site.

These are the types of sites Google has penalized in recent years with tweaks to its algorithms. (If you've heard of **Google Panda** and **Google Penguin**, those are the names Google gave to these tweaks.) It wants people searching Google to find sites that provide the information and products the searchers want.

This provides a great opportunity for legitimate business owners such as you. Right now, by combining high-quality content with legitimate white hat SEO techniques, you can make *both* your human visitors and search engine spiders happy.

When your copy is relevant, easy to read, and compelling — not just stuffed with irrelevant keywords to trick the spiders into ranking you more highly — you'll actually be increasing your SEO and receiving higher rankings (and thus increased traffic).

It's a lot harder to game the system now, and that's not a bad thing: It means legitimate websites such as yours are rising to the top while the tricksters are relegated to the depths of the SERPs.

As I mentioned earlier, even if those tricks work briefly in the short term, sites that use those tactics are massively penalized when they're found out. They can plummet so deep in search rankings that no one will ever see them, and when the tricks used are particularly egregious, Google (and Bing, and Yahoo) can even wipe the site out completely from search rankings — rendering the site essentially invisible.

If an Internet marketing "expert" claims he or she can substantially improve your site's rankings or traffic without making substantial improvements to the actual content, design, and relevance of the site, don't walk away — *run*. Trying to trick Google is a very, *very* bad idea. Instead, find a legitimate Internet marketing pro with a great white hat SEO record.

Great original content is great, but sham experts will rip off content from other sites and use it on yours. Relevant incoming and outgoing links are great, but these scammers will add links from hundreds of irrelevant websites.

They'll hook you into massive link exchange sites that provide nothing useful for your actual human visitors. The brief jump your site might see in rankings is not worth the damage that will occur when the hammer comes down.

Doing it the right way

So how do you do it the right way? It's important to understand what a search engine is looking for when determining how highly your site/landing page should rank in SERPs.

Though this relates to all major search engines, let's just use Google as an example. Every time someone does a search for certain keywords, Google's search engine considers the following:

Site authority: Is your site an authority on what the searcher is looking for? Having lots of high-quality, original content regarding the subject signals that it is. So do incoming links from other legitimate sites Google considers authoritative on the same subject. By filling your site with original content that informs and educates people on issues related to roofing — telling homeowners how to know whether they need a new roof, the newest innovations in techniques and materials, etc. — you're signaling to Google that you're an authority on the industry, while simultaneously establishing *trustworthiness* with human visitors that you'll take good care of their homes.

Social media: I'll discuss social media in general later in this book, but the more citations your site receives in social media, the more authoritative it appears on the subject.

Site performance: If your site receives lots of visitors, that's a big help. If those visitors not only stick around but also click on several other pages contained in the site, even better. Google tracks all these things, and they all affect your SEO.

Content: This doesn't just mean the words on the site. This means images, videos, and other media relevant to what the searcher is looking for. The more original the content, the better.

I like to say that *content is king*, and for good reason: More than anything these days, the quality of your content will determine how well (or how poorly) your site ranks.

Site design: Sites that are well designed are not only most helpful to human visitors, but to spiders as well. A well-designed site makes it easy for the spiders to interpret how relevant the site is to what people are looking for. A properly designed site also includes keywords in its image tags and coding to communicate relevance.

As for how to employ all these techniques and practices, that's a subject for a book that's much more comprehensive about SEO. You can use such resources to learn more about the specifics of determining what keywords to use in your copy and coding, designing your site for maximum impact on human visitors and spiders, and tracking how well your site is doing compared to your competitors. (Regularly analyzing and tweaking your approach is *absolutely necessary*.)

If, like most small business owners, you're more interested in concentrating your energies on running your business, a professional Internet marketing professional can handle all those elements for you. Just remember to be sure you find a provider who uses white hat tactics and can provide great examples of having increased sites' rankings through the legitimate methods detailed here.

Link building

As with SEO in general, link building is a broad subject. It's an essential part of SEO, because search engines place a huge amount of importance on which sites you link to (outgoing links) and which sites link to you (incoming links). If your roofing site is an island unto itself, that indicates to Google that your site is not very useful or influential, regardless of whether that's true.

That's why so much of black hat SEO is focused on artificially building up rankings based on link networks and purchased links. Not all link networks are necessarily "tricks," and not all purchased links are necessarily irrelevant, but they've been used so irresponsibly that it now requires great care to ensure you don't lead Google to believe you're up to no good.

When you build links appropriately and organically, you're employing a powerful tool for your site. I'll go over a few of the basics here:

In essence, every live webpage in existence has the ability to "vote" for other webpages by linking to them. How many votes are provided by an incoming link depends on several factors, but a key one is the SEO strength of the site that's voting.

How much the votes from that incoming link affect your SEO also can vary depending on the relevance of the linking website to yours (so getting inbound links from sites related to roofing, or at least home renovation and repair, is extremely useful), the content included in your link, and a few other things.

It's also important to consider **link velocity**, which refers to how quickly your site acquires new links. If your site gets hundreds or even thousands of new links in one fell swoop, that's far less beneficial than steadily aggregating links over a matter of time. The latter obviously indicates to Google that you're getting your links organically, whereas the former suggests a far less natural process.

The best way to get other sites to link to yours is to create useful, interesting content about the roofing industry. A blog that's specific to your main focus is thus incredibly beneficial for attracting links.

Post regularly with original copy that's relevant to sites you want to link to yours. Make sure the copy is clean and grammatically correct: No one wants to link to a site that reads like it was written by Yoda after a three-day bender.

Also, don't just write copy that sounds like you're pitching your company and services. While it's fine to mention your business on occasion, you're far more likely to attract incoming links if you're providing *solid information that's useful for everyone.*

Also, adding images, infographics, videos and other types of content specific to roofing makes your blog more SEO-attractive and engages readers.

Other ways to encourage links:

- **Make it easy for people to bookmark your posts and forward them to friends.** There are several tools that can be easily added to your site to allow people to do this with a single click. This is a great way to make posts go "viral" and gain links.

- **Include a link back to your website when you comment on other sites and blogs.** Most sites include a field for that, so use it. Obviously, be sure your comments are interesting and colorful, and that they represent your business in a professional manner. You obviously don't want a controversial comment — and especially not a crude or profane comment — linked to your business site.

- **Submit your site to directories.** There are many different directories — some free, some requiring a paid membership — that will be included as incoming links when you get listed with them. Obviously, be sure to list your site with directories that are specific to roofing, home repair and renovation, etc., along with your local chamber of commerce.

- **Link to other relevant sites whenever possible.** Reciprocal links are tricky. They aren't nearly as beneficial as other types when they appear to search engines to be a simply one-for-one trade. (That's similar to "I'll follow you if you follow me back" on Twitter.) However, in general, outgoing links help SEO when you're linking to quality sites, and sometimes those sites will link to you down the line. This will not hurt your SEO. Think of it as karma. Like the Beatles said, "the love you get is equal to the love you give."

<u>How to get in trouble</u>: If you want to take a chance of getting on the bad side of Google and Bing/Yahoo, the best way is to obtain incoming and outgoing links by buying and selling them.

Search engines — and yes, again it's Google in particular — do not like the selling of links at all. It sets off all sorts of alarms that something bogus is going on. Buying links, while not quite as dangerous as selling them, also has a tendency to backfire. Build your links naturally and organically.

As with SEO in general, there's more to generating great incoming links, but these are the basic tenets to keep in mind.

CHAPTER 2
Mobile Marketing

You'll recall that smartphones and tablets were mentioned somewhere in the vicinity of 150,000 times in the introduction.

Well, okay, maybe it wasn't quite that much. But I mentioned those technologies a lot, and honestly, there's no way to mention them too much. Because much like Internet marketing is marketing in this digital age, the mobile Internet isn't just the future — it's the present.

Even as I write this, smartphones and tablets are flying off the shelves. Of course they are. They're cheap, they're convenient, and they're incredibly useful. They're becoming a staple of everyday life.

Think about when you got your first cellphone. Suddenly, your landline didn't make a whole lot of sense anymore. You now had a phone in your hand that you could take anywhere. What use was it to have a phone that was wired to a wall in your home?

If you still have a landline in your home (one might still be useful in your roofing business, though perhaps not in this era of excellent Internet phone options), it likely serves as only as a complement to your mobile phone.

Similarly, the desktop computer is increasingly becoming only a complement to a laptop, smartphone, or tablet. Many people now access the Internet on these mobile technologies just as often as they do from home, if not more. In fact, the sales of personal computers (excluding tablets and other mobile devices) plunged in 2012, a trend that only accelerated throughout 2013. The desktop computer is starting to disappear from everyday life.

This is also a generational thing, of course. People under 30 are used to accessing information on the go. In your roofing business, these people might not yet comprise the bulk of your clientele, but they will do so increasingly over time. Kids today know how to operate an iPhone or Android phone before they even enter grade school. Young adults in their twenties and early thirties who are becoming homeowners have been accustomed to communicating through mobile technology for much of their lives.

And it's very important not to dismiss the effect of mobile technology on older generations. Ten years ago, you might not have expected people over 60 to be interested in carrying mobile phones. Now, many have abandoned their landlines and use their mobile phones exclusively.

Mobile marketing takes many forms, but in essence, it's simply the process of marketing and promoting your business through mobile technologies, whether through your website, social media, text messaging, or other means.

Defining a broad term

The concept of mobile marketing preceded the explosion in smartphone and tablet use, but the term had a more limited definition, for the most part, previously.

For example, the first thing many people thought of regarding the term mobile marketing was text messages, more specifically **SMS**, which stands for Short Message Service. This later expanded to **MMS** (Multimedia Message Service), which allows companies to text users who opt-in with images, audio, and video. Both technologies remain aspects of many companies' mobile marketing campaigns.

Another aspect was the innovation of **QR codes**, which allow a user to scan a 2D image with the phone's camera instead of typing in a URL or doing a Web search.

By including these images on posters, signs, magazine advertisements, etc., the company provides a simple way for the user to go straight to a website to access information or buy something.

However, today mobile marketing has taken on a broader definition. It now encompasses the type of marketing and promotion you would do for PC users, but for people now accessing the Internet on their phones.

For example, many websites are built to display well on laptop or desktop computer monitors. You can view them in the Google Chrome, Internet Explorer, or Mozilla Firefox browsers to ensure they display correctly.

Those same sites, however, display very differently when viewed on a smartphone. They can be hard to read and hard to navigate on smaller displays.

This has led many businesses to create mobile versions of their sites. The site knows it's being accessed from a mobile phone and defaults to a mobile version.

Other businesses take this process a step further and create Android or iOS apps for their phones, allowing the user to simply tap an app to access functions of the business.

Mobile marketing is *the* key tool for local businesses

Mobile marketing is most critical for businesses such as yours, who do all (or *virtually* all of their business) *locally*. Because you have a brick-and-mortar business that relies on local customers, it's critical to be sure your marketing efforts not only *include* mobile, but make it a *priority*.

It's time to stop thinking of your website or your online ads as being seen most often on a large monitor attached to a desktop computer.

Because you have a brick-and-mortar business that relies on local customers, it's critical to be sure your marketing efforts not only include mobile, but make it a priority.

Some people will be seeing it that way, sure, in the same way some people were still listening to audio cassettes when the rest of the world was moving to compact discs — and how a few stragglers are still listening to CDs today, even though the rest of the world has moved past physical media for listening to digital music.

Sure, your site should read well on a large screen, because it will be seen that way at times. But even just this year, considerably more people will be viewing it on a smartphone, and the numbers will just keep increasing in 2014 and 2015. Mobile SEO and Local SEO are virtually synonymous.

If your roofing business site isn't designed to automatically convert to a user-friendly mobile version when viewed on a phone, you'll lose virtually every customer who pulls it up on a smartphone. Not only does it take a lot more effort to read a full-featured site on a small screen, but you'll be seen by the visitor as hopelessly behind the times. If your local competitors have mobile-optimized sites and you don't, you're at a massive disadvantage.

As I note a couple of times elsewhere in this book, the great thing about mobile marketing is that you can market to people who are physically right down the street.

This doesn't just mean that they *live* right down the street. They could live an hour away, but if at the moment they're window shopping a few blocks away and wondering where they should get dinner, they can receive ads for a restaurant that the owner can push to all phones within a certain radius at a certain time. The owner could even push a happy hour ad right as happy hour is about to start.

Consider an auto repair service. Someone could have a CV joint on his car snap a few blocks away. When he checks his map app for the closest auto repair shops, that repair shop will pop up — presuming the owner has taken the time to properly fill out her information in the listings.

She could include information such as "free tow within five miles — free estimate for no extra charge" on her site, but she could also push an ad with that message to mobile phones within a five-mile radius.

Mobile devices also make it extremely easy to monitor statistics on who's checking out your site and listings, when and where they're viewing it, and which visitors chose to contact you or otherwise convert into a customer. These analytics are critical to optimizing your marketing campaign.

Looking forward in mobile marketing

Because smartphones have only in the past couple of years become so widespread among every demographic — though that's happening *really* fast right now — we're really still in the nascence of mobile marketing technology. But the possibilities appear endless.

Consider that virtually everyone is (or soon will be) carrying around a super-powered computer that doubles as a two-way communication device, with GPS and WiFi technology that provides location information on a regular basis.

This is why mobile marketing will continue to be the big thing in the years to come. Billboards simply seek to catch the attention of eyeballs. Mobile marketing seeks the attention of something that's becoming far more important: a person's personal, handheld technological lifeline.

According to a 2010 study by Google, advertisers experience, on average, an 11.5 percent increase in mobile click-through rates when they run a mobile-specific campaign (as compared to a hybrid or PC-only campaign).

And remember, that was in *2010*. Even in 2013 and as we enter 2014, mobile advertising is one of the *most inexpensive* forms of online advertising.

Experts predict that there will be more than 85 percent smartphone adoption among all Americans within 2–3 years. Mobile SEO is going to make or break certain types of companies.

CHAPTER 3
Social Media Marketing

Some people would argue the world was a better place when people could sit down in a restaurant and could resist the urge to look down at their phones every 30 seconds to see whether they had a new notification on Facebook or a new tweet on Twitter.

Actually, there's a lot to be said for that argument. Regardless, that situation is a reality these days, especially with younger generations. Some people say they're addicted to their phones, and it's hard to disagree. They communicate constantly through social media, and that communication, as noted earlier, increasingly occurs through phones and tablets.

The two (current) giants in social media, Facebook and Twitter, wield astonishing power to let people and businesses interact with each other in real time. Having a major presence on these two platforms is a requirement for any online business. That's less the case for certain types of businesses, but one thing is inarguable: No matter what product you sell or service you provide, you can benefit from using social media. It's just as important in the roofing industry (or any "physical" business) as it is for companies that work exclusively in the cloud.

The biggest benefit to platforms such as Facebook and Twitter, along with other major players such as Pinterest, is the cost: their basic functions are free. Sure, there are paid advertising functions that can be used as desired, but it costs nothing to set up a basic Facebook page and start posting. Same with Twitter. They provide a means to reach out to both current and potential customers at no included cost.

Of course, money isn't the only valuable resource to a business. Time is just as valuable, and the time expended on social media is a factor in its use. Your business might be set up in a way where you can easily communicate regularly on Facebook or Twitter on a daily basis.

If it isn't, you might need to delegate those responsibilities to an employee or contract the process out, and those options require financial resources.

Whatever the case, every business should have a company page on Facebook at the very least. It's simply expected in today's digital world. Having a Facebook page — and making sure to post on it regularly, even if it's only a short post or two every day — show that you're active and engaged in today's digital world.

Every time your company adds friends/followers on Facebook or Twitter, you're adding to the company's profile and influence. Every time you blog about subjects relevant to roof replacement/repair and people comment on the posts or link to them, you're expanding your outreach.

However, there's one critical thing to understand whenever you use social media to market your business: If you use it unwisely — being too focused on pitching your business or spamming followers with commercial links — you're risking a massive backlash. There are few better ways to sink your social media marketing than by being too commercially oriented.

That might sound strange, given that your whole reason for social marketing is to increase awareness, traffic, clientele, and sales, but it's a quirk of social media.

It's critical to understand that people don't use social media to be "sold to." They use it to interact and to learn about things of interest to them. There's a lot of room *within that construct* to promote your business, but for the most part, it has to be done *without a hard sell*.

Use social media to make connections with interested parties. Share information, resources, advice, suggestions. You're a professional in roof replacement and repair, so put that knowledge to use. When people show interest in your products or services, that's the time to provide such useful information.

Social media can be an incredibly useful resource for business marketing when used wisely, but it can backfire quickly if you let the temptation of the hard sell get in the way.

Build relationships first; sell later.

Is this new social network worth the time?

Not every social media platform is equal. Facebook and Twitter are superstars of the social media world, at least for now, and LinkedIn and Google+ aren't far behind. (To be honest, Google+ definitely has some catching up to do, but Google is constantly combining its social media aspect with all its tools, so Google+ will only continue to gain prominence). But those are only four among the hundreds of social media platforms trying to gain your participation, your involvement, and hopefully (for them), your business.

There are only so many hours in the day, and as a small business owner, you need to be able to tell the wheat from the chaff. We've put together a few questions you should consider when determining whether a new social network will drive leads and make your phone ring.

Who is using the network now? Not who the platform wants to use the network. Not who it hopes will use the network. Who is on there *currently*?

You should be able to identify the demographics of the network, how and when its users are interacting with it, why they are using it, and how involved they are.

Demographics is a big consideration: For example, the Pinterest platform is composed of 80 percent female users. Almost 30 percent of users are ages 25–34.

Are those demographics relevant targets for your business? One could argue that they are. That's a big demographic for first-time homeowners, and it's fair to say that the home aesthetics are typically as important to female homeowners as it is to male homeowners.

Additionally, Pinterest is inherently a visual social platform. While it might not seem immediately obvious how important this could be for a roofing business, there are possibilities.

For example, you could post images that show the damage and wear people should look out for on their homes' roofs. You could post before-and-after images of roofs you've replaced and/or repaired. Pinterest provides a simple way to show off your services visually.

How likely are these people to use or promote your product? Even if the people using the network fall into your demographic, you need to determine whether they're likely to be interested in becoming your roofing customers — or at least whether they're likely to promote your products/services through word of mouth.

Are these the type of people using the platform? Is the platform itself set up to easily share items of interest between people using it? The networks that provide the best return on investment tend to be the ones in which social sharing elements are integral to the platform and consistently used.

Do you have the content/resources/time to participate meaningfully in this particular network? If a particular business doesn't (or can't) produce videos, YouTube isn't of much use. However, it can be a boon for someone in your line of work. Video provides a great way to showcase the transformation process of putting in a new roof. The prospective customer doesn't just have to mentally visualize the change: A well-shot video brings the entire process to life.

Is it worth it to you to produce content specifically for that network? Content creation requires time and (sometimes) money. You don't want to fall in the trap of buying or duplicating content, which can often backfire, so you'll need something original.

The more networks you join, the more time you'll spend, and the more likely you are to post only sporadically on each. It's generally better to focus your efforts on a few key networks that fit your business and make sure to regularly contribute to those platforms.

Facebook

You know your creation has become a landmark aspect of popular culture when someone makes a major feature film about both your creation and you. *The Social Network* might not have always portrayed Facebook inventor Mark Zuckerberg in the kindest light, but the film's very existence showed what a gigantic influence Facebook is in people's everyday lives.

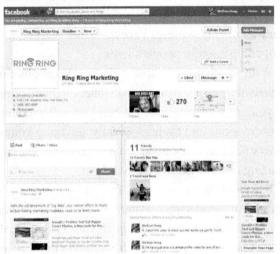

Speaking of movies, there's a moment in the 1991 Madonna film *Truth or Dare* where Madonna's friend, actor Warren Beatty, says of the pop star: "She doesn't want to live off-camera, much less talk. There's nothing to say off-camera. Why would you say something if it's off-camera? What point is there in existing?"

To Beatty's mind, Madonna (at least in 1991) didn't see any worth in something happening if it wasn't filmed. Similarly, many young people today think there's only worth in something if they post it on Facebook or tweet about it. If it's not communicated to the world (or at least their friends), how much worth can it have?

You can love or hate that fact, but it speaks to the power Facebook holds. Mobile technology allows people to access Facebook constantly. When you're tagged in a post or someone messages you, your phone (if it's set up that way, as most are) sends you a notification immediately. With an astonishing *800 million active users* as of this writing, Facebook has become a constant companion in people's lives.

With all that said, how effective Facebook social engagement will be for your business depends greatly on your type of business. When you sell products or do promotions and events — really, anything your customers need to know about on a regular basis — it's an amazing tool for getting the word out.

Facebook is an incredible free promotion tool. Post pictures of your happy customers outside their homes with their great new roofs. Advise your followers about times you might be closed for remodeling (or just a well-deserved vacation). Offer discounts for people who mention specific posts that appear on your page. This is different from a hard-sell approach: It's providing value to people who frequent your establishment.

Advertising on Facebook: The social engagement aspect of Facebook is obviously useful, but again, it has its limitations, such as the need to avoid a hard-sell approach. Facebook paid advertising is an entirely different animal. The platform provides tools that allow you to place ads that will conform to people's interests across Facebook.

This isn't a good place to get into the specifics, for two reasons. First, it can be a bit complicated. Second, Facebook revises its advertising approach constantly, so best practices today could be very different by next week.

Whether Facebook advertising will provide a good return on your investment is something to consider thoughtfully, preferably with the assistance of an Internet marketing professional.

Facebook Fan Page vs. Standard Facebook page: The word "fan" throws some people off here, because you wouldn't typically ask your customers to become "fans" of your business per se.

However, a fan page is exactly what you want for your business. It differentiates the entity that is your business from you as an individual. You can apply different controls to the page, what people are allowed to post, and so on.

You don't want to use your personal Facebook page for your roofing business. These should remain separate entities. Your personal friends won't necessarily be interested in the commercial status updates needed for your business, and your companies' "fans" don't necessarily want your personal posts showing up on their timelines.

Keeping your professional and personal Facebook pages separate (although they can "Like" each other, of course) is the only way to go. You can also focus on various strategies of improving SEO specifically for your business's Facebook Fan Page, along with possibly considering paying for sponsored posts, as detailed in the following section.

Sponsored posts on Facebook

If you have any type of business, having some sort of presence on Facebook is a must. It's a largely simple and completely free way to build your brand, market your services, and communicate to your customers.

Actually, let's get back to that "completely free" thing for the moment. Yes, it's still completely free, but as with any very successful social media platform — particularly one still reeling from a recent less-than-impressive initial public offering — Facebook is looking to monetize its services.

If you use Facebook, you've probably noticed the recently added ability to "promote" your posts.

Facebook has allowed businesses to promote their posts for some time now, but it's now branched out that option to person users. Promotion allows you to increase the time your post is seen by your friends, in addition to increasing the likelihood the post will be seen.

It's hard to see how much this will benefit a business owner. Sure, there might be times when reaching out to everyone on your friends list in a more visible way is beneficial, such as when you have a big sale or marketing event coming up.

However, it's pretty early in the process to know whether the return on investment will be sufficient. It's something to watch as the post-promotion initiative goes forward.

Facebook Graph Search:
What you need to know

This innovation was released in early 2013, and it's proven to be worth the huge buzz even as we enter 2014. The important question, of course: What is it?

It's basically a new search engine that works inside Facebook. It's currently in its beta stage, so Facebook users can join in after getting on a wait list.

You're likely familiar with the very basic Facebook search we've come to know and... not so much love. There's not much to it. To find a friend or business, you punch in a name. However, you invariably get a lot of hits that are not the person or place you're looking for. So you scroll through them and hopefully, eventually, find what you're looking for.

That's why Facebook launched Graph Search: to make the Facebook search experience much easier and more efficient. It's actually powered by Microsoft's Bing search engine, which — while not as popular as Google Search — works well and has many advantages of its own.

In a nutshell, the search function pulls up much more relevant information that's based on you — your interests, your pastimes, what you care about.

By doing this, you receive results that are far more likely to align with what (and whom) you're looking for. There are similarities between this and Google+, but Facebook remains far more popular for social interaction than Plus does.

Facebook is hoping that instead of simply using Google Search to find businesses and people of interest to you, you'll use its Graph Search function, which it believes will get you what you're looking for faster and much more efficiently.

While how this will all shake out has yet to be seen (as the function moves out of beta and becomes widely adopted), there's no question that having powerful interests such as Facebook and Microsoft behind it means that Graph Search will become a big player in online search.

For now, what it means to your local roofing business is that you should ensure you're active and well represented on Facebook, both on your own page and in interacting with users. That will increase the likelihood that people using Graph Search will find your business.

Not only that, but you'll be prequalified by "Likes" from those users' friends and people within their fields of interest.

What can Facebook Graph do for you?

For most of its life, Facebook has had a very primitive search function, not that it's exactly stymied the network's growth. But the launch of Graph Search in January 2013 shook things up considerably, providing users the ability to search numerous aspects of its members' personal data.

The focus is on four different categories: people, photos, places, and interests. What's cool about Graph Search is how it weights aspects that are similar to those of people (or businesses) to which you're connected on Facebook. For example, places that your connections "Like" or perform a check-in will show up higher on your Graph Search.

The changes to Facebook's search function make the platform much more useful for marketing purposes, but as a Facebook user, you should also be aware that it makes information you might have considered private — or at least information you didn't necessarily want to broadcast to the world — far more easily accessible.

If you've "Liked" certain pages without much consideration, be advised that a Graph Search can show all that info unless you've restricted that information in your privacy settings. Similarly, if people have restricted that information in their own settings, you won't get "hits" for them when you perform a search.

On the other hand, you should use the Graph Search function to make sure that everything you want users to find when they search for local roofers will show up. You need to get your social profile in order.

Graph Search and Facebook's other new product, Nearby, are expected to make the social network a major player in user-friendly local searches, giving Yelp, Google, and Foursquare a run for their collective money.

Going forward, your approach needs to change related to your business on Facebook. In the past, brand content and updates were vital to stay relevant within your timeline and to provide exposure for your news feed.

With the introduction of Graph Search, the importance of those updates has been lowered dramatically. Ranking within Graph Search is all about *social connections.*

Graph search even has *Photos* as its own category now. So that means encouraging your fans, customers, and others to check in, recommend, rate, and add photos to your pages is that much more important going forward. (That's more than enough reason to ask a happy client to share a picture of a gorgeous new roof you installed.)

Why? Because these social connections are pretty much the "links" that Facebook uses to determine relevancy and authority. It's these photos, likes, check-ins, recommendations, etc. that the Graph Search algorithm will use to qualify and personalize results for Facebook users.

In a very real sense, "Likes" (and "+1's" on Google+) are becoming the "links" of the new digital era. What you Like defines you (and/or your business).

Twitter

When Twitter arrived on the scene, business owners were originally skeptical about how useful this tool could be. If all you can do is post something in 140 characters, how useful can that be?

However, a number of tools have made Twitter much more useful for businesses, including options that allow you to write longer posts (with the remainder represented by a link), link shorteners, promoted accounts and posts, and other improvements.

At its heart, Twitter provides a great opportunity to communicate with customers in real time. Because most people use Twitter on their phones, you can connect with followers when they're out and about.

Because the people who see your tweets are people who already follow you (or have retweeted your tweets to *their* followers), you have a largely prequalified audience for your tweets. And, of course, just like Facebook, it's totally free to tweet anytime you like. (Promoted posts, of course, cost money.)

Advertising options for Twitter include **promoted tweets**, which let you promote your brand by targeting users who are similar to your current followers and those who have searched terms related to your product. **Promoted accounts** appear in the "who to follow" section and in search results, appearing on the pages of users that would likely be interested in your brand.

There are other options as well, but what's right for you will depend on what you're looking to achieve.

Even if you don't use Twitter's paid options, it's an amazing way not only to communicate with your clientele, but also to receive immediate feedback. People who won't take the time to send an email are happy to fire off a quick tweet to let you know their feelings about your products and services.

Also, happy customers can provide great word of mouth in seconds by tweeting to their friends whenever they have a great experience. If someone does have a bad experience and posts about it on Twitter, at least you'll know about it right away and have an opportunity to make it right.

Yelp

Yelp was one of the first platforms to mix user reviews with a social media aspect, and it remains one of the biggest. With well over 70 million monthly unique visitors, its influence is enormous. Throughout its existence, it's at times been an enormous benefit to local businesses — and also a huge pain in the butt. Most businesses have experienced both sides of the coin.

The concept is simple: After people go to local businesses — a doughnut shop, a motorcycle repair shop, a fine restaurant — they post a review on Yelp. These reviews help other people decide whether to frequent the establishment.

If every single Yelp user took care to provide a fair, unbiased, thoughtful review of the particular business, everything would be hunky-dory. You could read through the reviews and determine which ones you felt were most accurate and legitimate.

However, like everything else on the Internet, people will try to game the system. Some people try to get perks from the establishments in exchange for a positive review. Some business owners try to run down their competitors with unfairly critical reviews, simply making up facts as they go.

And some people, even if they're not trying to game the system per se, just don't take the time to be very thoughtful when reviewing an establishment. If they just happened to be having a bad day, they might rip apart a place (figuratively) even if everything actually was satisfactory.

Yelp has taken steps to deal with all of these issues, and how effective those steps have been might depend on your perspective. The company says it has systems in place to help weed out bogus reviews and keep them from being posted.

Such bogus reviews, of course, are not only negative: Business owners have been known to sign up with several different accounts and review their own establishments — with glowing reviews across the board, of course.

The ascendancy of smartphones and tablets — you knew they were going to come up again — has only made Yelp more powerful. Its local search capabilities make it easy to find places near where you are at a given moment and see reviews for those places. You can see why the veracity of those reviews is so incredibly important to business owners.

With all the concern about the veracity of Yelp pages, is it worth it to even participate in the process?

The answer is yes. Online reviews are not going away, and neither is Yelp. People are going to review your company one way or another, and by getting involved, you can help ensure you're being seen in the best light.

As you well know, people aren't going to contract to have a new roof installed on a whim. They'll want to have plenty of information before signing off on home renovations and inviting people into their home to do the work.

It goes without saying that having several excellent reviews on the Internet's top review site gives you a *gigantic* advantage over local competitors who have negative reviews or simply too-few reviews. This alone can be the difference between convincing homeowners to contract with you over other local options. That's why you cannot afford to ignore your reputation on Yelp (or other major review sites).

If you believe a review of your business is plainly factually inaccurate or clearly bogus, Yelp has tools to let you ask for it to be removed. That might not always happen, but at least there's a process.

If you simply think a review was overly harsh (but not necessarily objectively inaccurate), you can reach out to the user and try to get to the root of the problem. By communicating respectfully with the reviewer and addressing the concerns, you'll often get a new review from the user that's much more positive.

There's nothing wrong with encouraging your satis-fied customers to post positive reviews about your business, but here is where I should provide a caveat: Yelp itself is not a fan of this practice. To Yelp, this gets a little too close to "buying" reviews, which is absolutely *verboten* — and can get you stamped with an unsavory label on the site for some time.

If a customer tells you she was ecstatic with the great job you did, I think it's fine to suggest she post a review on Yelp if she'd like. It's more precarious to offer incentives for people who post reviews. Never require a five-star review, for example, in return for a benefit you provide. That can very easily backfire — you don't want to be seen as effectively bribing reviewers. Simply speak with customers who you know loved the roofing work you did and politely ask for a review.

The root of getting great Yelp reviews is simple: Do a great job. Provide great customer service, listen to any concerns from customers, and show that you deserve great reviews. The best reviews come from customers who loved their experience and decide on their own that they'd like to pass on the word.

Handling negative Yelp reviews

Yelp has proven to be a great service for promoting your local business's service and products. (Though its newest foray into paid listings has more questionable benefits, as we'll discuss later.) It's an easy way to benefit from great word-of-mouth by your customers and show off the excellent customer service you provide.

That is, of course, if you're receiving positive reviews. If you're getting hit with negative reviews — whether fair or unfair — on your Yelp site, that can throw a serious monkey wrench into the process. People naturally pay more attention to negative reviews than positive ones, and you don't want those criticisms to define your business to potential customers.

What can you do if you get negative reviews? That depends on the particular review. First, let's focus on reviews that are unfair or violate Yelp's terms of service.

In this case, you have two options: You can go to yelp.com/contact and select Questionable Content. This isn't the fastest option, but you will receive a direct reply from Yelp's customer support team. Alternatively, you can flag the review. This will be handled more quickly, but you won't receive a response regarding the issue's resolution.

Let's say you receive a negative review that you can't necessarily contest through Yelp. Perhaps the reviewer has a legitimate gripe about your business, or perhaps it's simply a matter of miscommunication.

One option is to reach out to the customer through a private message. Always be positive and professional when you do this. You can note any positive aspects the customer mentioned, apologize for the problem, try to rectify the issue and welcome the customer to try your services again.

Another good option is to make a public comment on the review. Again, always be *positive* and *professional*. You can address the concerns noted and specify any changes you've made to address the problem. How you respond to the review will go a long way in determining how other visitors think of your business, so a calm, diplomatic response is highly advised.

Also, keep in mind that if the comment reads like it was written by a troll, visitors are savvy enough to recognize that. When it's been reviewed enough times, every great business will still get a handful of one-star reviews. You don't have to respond to every one, but when you do, be sure you're the one taking the high road.

Yelp paid ads: sound investment or rip-off?

As we noted earlier, Yelp can be a huge boon to your local business. If you don't have a listing on Yelp, you're missing out on a key opportunity to promote your local roofing company and leverage the power of customer reviews.

Taping letters from happy customers to your wall only communicates your great customer service to people inside your front door — and they're already your clientele. Having those great reviews posted on your Yelp page gets the word out to everyone.

However, the picture has become muddied recently by Yelp's foray into paid advertising. Yelp is promoting this new initiative as a way to trump your competitors by giving your Yelp page better visibility. Sounds great, right? In reality, many marketing experts are suggesting that Yelp's paid ads currently cost far more than what you receive in return.

The numbers can get a little confusing if you're not familiar with cost per impressions, which is the model Yelp is using for the ads. Much like traditional advertising, an impression merely means that someone has seen your ad. You're paying for the ad regardless of whether or not someone clicks through to your site. Cost-per-click, by comparison, only costs you money if someone clicks through.

With Yelp ads, the cost per impression (CPM) is exponentially more expensive than it is with standard CPM advertising. It's also much harder to track how effective your advertising is when you can't get click-through numbers. Yelp is also requiring a one-year commitment for its most favorable rates, which aren't particularly low in the first place.

When you add it up, it doesn't make a lot of sense to pay for Yelp advertising at this time, though that might change if the platform makes some changes to its business model (and its pricing) in the future.

Blogging

The benefits of having a business blog are almost too great to mention. Blogging about issues related to roofing (and other matters related to home improvement, repair and renovation) in a way that displays expertise provides you enormous credibility, which goes a long way in your industry. It lets you communicate about what's going on with your company. It provides people the opportunity to provide feedback and ask questions through comments.

(And you can moderate those comments before they're posted, removing the risk of spam or other problems.)

Then there's the SEO consideration: When you're generating a lot of content for your website that's relevant to roofing, your SEO increases *massively*. Having a strong, regularly updated blog is one of the very best things you can do to increase your website's traffic and search engine rankings.

Blogging also helps you create incoming and outgoing links, which are great for SEO. You can (and should) link to other relevant sites and articles in your blog posts. There's plenty of information about roofing out there, and your clientele surely will be interested in other home improvement topics as well — feel free to expand the range to target their interests. When you post something of interest to others, it's likely your post will be linked to (or shared through other platforms), increasing your incoming links and traffic to your site.

With all that said, there are some obvious potential downsides to blogging. Spelling, grammatical, or factual errors in your posts can make you look unprofessional, so if you're not a good writer (or sufficiently detail-oriented), you should have a better-suited employee or a contracted professional do your blogging for you.

Alternately, you might be a great writer, but you just don't have time to blog. That's another reason to consider delegating the posting process. Whatever the case, the benefit to blogging is almost always worth finding a way to make it work.

Another concern relates to content. Many websites have gotten in trouble (appropriately) with Google for simply duplicating content from other sites in their blog posts. Not only is this unethical (and in certain circumstances, illegal), but it's a great way to prompt Google, Yahoo, or Bing to drop your search engine ranking into the sewer.

Let's take a second to underline that point: *Don't copy content from other sites.* You also shouldn't buy content that clearly wasn't originally written for your site. Even if you change around a few words here or there or "spin" the copy (a computerized process that rewords sentences), Google has ways of finding it out.

Write original content whenever possible. Posts don't necessarily have to be long; even a couple of paragraphs can be enough, as long as the content is focused on roof installation and repair, or on subjects related to that field.

If you want to share information from another site, no problem: Simply write a sentence or two in a post and link to the site where the article or post appears. You can even excerpt a small amount of the other post, but the key word in that sentence is *small*; too much will get you in trouble. And whenever you use some-one else's content in an excerpt, be certain to include attribution and a link.

As with everything else, blogging is more beneficial for certain types of businesses and services than others, but it has some benefits no matter what you do. Just its ability to improve your site's SEO alone is a good rea-son to try it. If it sounds like too great a time investment, speak with a marketing consultant about possible options to outsource the process.

A lot of people make their livings blogging for a variety of different sites, and depending on your needs, these services can be very affordable, especially given the return on investment.

LinkedIn

A social network specifically for business professionals: a simple enough concept, and one that's worked out for LinkedIn to the tune of more than 200 million members. Don't get too hung up the term "business professionals." You don't need to wear a suit and tie to work to benefit from LinkedIn. That's how pervasive it has become for business networking.

LinkedIn simply makes it incredibly easy to allow registered users to maintain a list of contact details for people with whom they have some level of relationship. These people are called **connections**.

Once you've made connections, you can connect with people connected to them, allowing you to easily expand your networking base with people in your industry or with common interests/work histories.

You can create a comprehensive profile with a full resume and qualifications, and when you're looking for a new employee or business partner, you can search through LinkedIn users for the experience, skills, and qualifications you're looking for.

LinkedIn also allows you to endorse people you've worked with — and be endorsed by the same — with the click of a button. Having your business and various skills endorsed by well-connected users is obviously a great way to gain new business and new opportunities.

Here's the usual caveat: LinkedIn is most beneficial for businesses in which professional networking is an integral part of doing business. However, the platform has a lot of additional tools that can be useful for virtually every type of business owner.

LinkedIn doesn't require constant participation, though the more you participate on the platform, the more helpful it can be. At the very least, having a LinkedIn profile for yourself is a great way to put your best foot forward and display your roofing skills and experience to people who might not otherwise know about them.

For a roofing business, linking to other providers in the industry and those who provide related services (albeit not necessarily your competitors) can provide a great foundation for organically building incoming links. When their sites link to yours, it can improve your traffic and greatly improve your organic SEO, because Google values incoming links from companies in your field very highly.

Google+ Business

I touched upon Google+ before, but it's useful to note it briefly here as well, because Google+ is, at its heart, a social network.

Your Google+ Business page is your virtual business identity in the Google universe. To be able to interact in the Google social network and have followers share your business, you need to have your Google+ Business identity set up and ready to share.

These listings already integrate such things as Zagat ratings, Street View, and Google Plus user ratings, letting your Google+ Business listing do everything your Yelp page does. Google Local and Maps only add to the functionality.

What's especially beneficial for Google+ Business is that Google knows much more about each of its individual users' preferences than Yelp ever will.

Hangouts: While it might not be the first term that comes to mind regarding a professional business, the Hangouts initiative is a key aspect to how Google is merging its business functionality with the social aspect of Google+.

Google Hangouts provides a simple means by which you can invite customers into your business, basically like having an open house in the virtual world, using high-quality, easy-to-use video chat.

This chapter covered the basics of several top platforms in social media, but that's just the tip of the iceberg.

Many business owners are wary of social media because they assume it takes up too much time, but when used thoughtfully and wisely, it's a key aspect of any successful marketing campaign in today's world.

CHAPTER 4
Online Deals / Coupon Sites

I'll keep the introduction to this one pretty short, because the chapter title pretty much says it all: online deals and coupon sites are exactly what you'd expect them to be. They're very similar to the coupons you'll find in the newspaper (if you still get one) or in your mailbox (and with online billing and statements these days, those mailed coupons might be most of the mail you currently get, at least at home).

There are some differences, of course, and not just that your scissors probably last a lot longer than they used to now that you don't have to spend so much time cutting along those dotted lines.

Many online coupons and deals have different considerations. They can have different types of expiration periods. Some don't actually take effect unless a certain number of people opt-in to the deal. Also, many require that you actually purchase the product or service at the discounted rate up front.

Because this book is written for the business owner's perspective, the object here is to determine whether getting involved with an online deal or coupon is a good investment for your business. For a roofing business, an online deal or coupon can provide a fast way to gain a lot of new customers. On the other hand — and obviously this is a major consideration — you'll have to discount your standard price substantially to participate.

Note: All the online coupon/daily deals providers skyrocketed for a couple of years, but for the past two years or so, they've seen revenues *plummet*. This indicates that the daily deal concept, at least the way it's currently being employed, might not stick around for the long run. With that in mind, here are the major players:

Groupon

This is probably the first name that comes to mind when you think about online coupons. It became incredibly popular incredibly quickly, having launched in November 2008.

In fewer than two years, it already had more than 35 million registered users. (It's worth noting, however, that a small percentage of those users regularly take advantage of the site's deals.) The company went public in 2012, but its valuation was weaker than expected after its IPO.

Groupon, of course, doesn't actually sell anything. It provides a platform through which businesses can offer a deal to potential customers at a (typically very steep) discount. For this, Groupon earns a negotiated percentage of the discounted price people paid for the deal.

The upside to Groupon is that a business doesn't have to pay anything up front or do (relatively) any work in marketing its deal. Groupon handles all of that. When you do a Groupon for a local business, the company will promote the deal to people in your local area, and it uses other metrics to target people who would be interested in your type of product or service. Groupon naturally wants as many people as possible to purchase the deal, because that's where it makes its money.

However, the typical structure of a Groupon deal doesn't make it easy for the business to make money. Your standard margins have to be pretty high to make money off a Groupon deal. The company typically requires that you cut your standard pricing by *50 percent* or more, and Groupon effectively splits the remaining profits with you. (Individual deals vary, but this is by far the most common arrangement.)

That means a business owner is looking at clearing at best 25 percent of your standard pricing after the discount and Groupon's take. Long story short, businesses that actually profited off a Groupon deal are few and far between.

So why do a Groupon deal? The main reason is obvious: It introduces people to your service or product and hopefully widens your base of regular customers. If your local roofing company has a hard time attracting new customers or can't afford the up-front cost of advertising, it's a way to attract customers without the big outlay. You're only paying Groupon each time someone actually takes advantage of the deal, after all.

However, studies have indicated that the return customer rate for Groupon deals isn't very impressive. Groupon has indicated a *22 percent* return rate, while independent research has shown substantially lower numbers.

People who purchase Groupons tend to be attracted to deals, but they're far less likely to contract with you again once you're back to charging your standard rate.

There are certain circumstances in which a Groupon could be beneficial. If you need to get rid of over-stocked merchandise and would be deeply discounting it anyway, Groupon could be a useful vehicle. It's also helpful if you're looking for exposure for your business without a big financial outlay.

Also, if you commonly run big discounts on your roofing materials products or services anyway, you might see a better return rate, because this is exactly the audience you're looking for.

<u>LivingSocial</u>

LivingSocial is Groupon's biggest competitor, and like Groupon, it experienced tremendous growth right out of the gate, followed by a number of financial setbacks.

It's a private company, so it doesn't share its financial information publicly, but Amazon (a large stakeholder in the company) announced a $650 million net loss for its holdings in LivingSocial for 2012. The company laid off 400 employees in November 2012 after a 94 percent dropoff in revenues over the previous 11 months.

LivingSocial, which claims more than 70 million users, works in very much the same fashion as Groupon, so I won't belabor those points. LivingSocial refers to its offerings as Daily Deals instead of coupons.

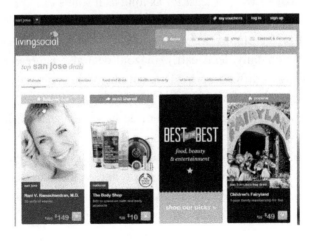

One difference is that many business owners who tried both have noted better customer service experiences with LivingSocial than with Groupon, and though those reports are anecdotal, there are enough reports that it's something to consider. Also, LivingSocial's partnership with Amazon gives it some extra exposure, which I'll touch on in a minute.

Virtually all of the same pros and cons regarding Groupon relate to LivingSocial, so let them be your guide. With either company, unless your standard prices are already inflated, profit will be hard to come by. Exposure is the greatest benefit of these companies.

AmazonLocal

One thing that might keep LivingSocial from going under is its aforementioned partnership with Amazon, which has the money and power to keep anything afloat — well, at least for as long as it wants to.

Amazon jumped into the daily deal arena in mid-2011, before the wheels started to come off the online coupon/daily deals cart. AmazonLocal also aggregates deals by different providers, but one of the main ones it includes is LivingSocial.

AmazonLocal's version of daily deals doesn't differ much from Groupon or LivingSocial. As with those two, it doesn't charge an upfront fee for the service, just a commission. It's safe to say the pros and cons are fairly similar for this service, though the Amazon platform — because it's being used as an umbrella to opt-in people who are Amazon customers already — could be a benefit.

Google Offers

Here's where I tell you that Google Offers is completely different from the other daily deals options.

Just kidding. It's the same thing. Same business model, same general advantages and disadvantages for businesses.

That said, there are a few factors that favor the Google option, if you're definitely interested in running some type of deal. Google's Android has become the most popular smartphone operating system, and that, when married with Google's massive popularity in applications such as Google+ Local and Maps, is a real benefit.

For example, the Google Maps compatibility allows users to discover deals when they search for local businesses. Google Offers allows businesses to offer something free (like a free dessert when you buy an entree), helping give potential customers an extra nudge.

Your type business certainly isn't going to provide something as substantial as an entire new roof for free, but if you have an associated service (such as minor-to-moderate roof repair) that's inexpensive, this might be an avenue to consider.

Google also claims it has better payment deals for its offers than the other providers offer, so that's something to consider. With the daily deals arena falling on hard times in general, if you needed to bet on a horse to win, Google isn't a bad choice.

Ultimately, if you're interested in an online coupon/daily deal offer, it's best to check around with all the providers and find the best options for you.

If the numbers just won't add up, it's best to consider other options. However, if getting broad exposure even at the cost of massively reduced prices isn't a great concern, a daily deal option might be a useful venture.

Section 2:

Conversions

CHAPTER 5
Maximizing Website Conversions

Internet marketing *is* marketing.

Sound familiar? No, you haven't accidentally begun reading the book from the start again. I just wanted to mention it again, because it leads to the next point.

In this digital age, just as Internet marketing *is* marketing, a website *is* your business's home. You might think your business's home is its actual physical office, and for a roofing business, you obviously need a brick-and-mortar location, if only for supplies and equipment (and probably more, depending on the size of your business).

Regardless, you also need a business address in the *cloud*, which is another way of saying you need a website. You must have actual official space on the Web. It's as crucial as having an office. Your business could change its *physical* location many times, but its website is a constant, the place where anyone can find you in this digital age.

In the digital age, where you and your business are physically only matters so much. Where you exist *online* matters a great deal.

Perhaps you're thinking: So what? I have a website. I pay a few bucks every year or two to the domain provider and hosting company. My phone number is on there, a picture of the business, maybe even a couple of

paragraphs about what we do. I've done my due dili-
gence.

Well, that's the bare minimum. That's like putting
on shoes because the grocery store won't serve you
otherwise. Simply having a website is like simply having a business. It exists. Now what are you going to do
with it?

Like every other aspect of your business, your website has a purpose. We can refer to that purpose in general ways, such as building your brand, listing testimonials and reviews, displaying pictures of work you've
done, that sort of thing. But it all ultimately comes
down to one thing: **conversions**.

People define the term a lot of different ways. For
businesses where the goal is online sales, a conversion
is a very simple thing: a sale. It's *converted* a visitor
into a paying customer.

As a local roof installer, you likely earn your revenue through providing services in person. In that situation, it's not as easy to gauge how effective your web-

site has been in converting visitors by using basic sales analytics.

However, there are many analytical methods to determine how effective your website is at attracting new visitors and determining how they got there, how long they spend on the site, what pages they click on, and how long they spend on those pages. These tools allow you to see what images, videos, and links they click on. All these tools allow you to know what's working — and what's not — in appealing to new customers.

I've said it before, and I'll say it again: People are now shopping online far more than ever before. They're finding businesses and services online. If they want to find a dog walker, a bike shop, or a psychic, they're finding them *online*.

Businesses that have no website at all? They're in massive trouble. To the ever-growing digital population, those businesses don't exist.

Businesses that have a bare-bones website? They're almost as invisible as those with *no* website. With little-to-no content, no SEO to attract visitors, no incoming links to provide inroads for potential customers, a website like that is a needle in the proverbial haystack.

Businesses with a middle-of-the-road website? That's 100 times better, no question about it. If it has some content, some degree of SEO, and uses some links — and if that's tied in with a touch of social media — that website is actually achieving the minimum standard of what's needed to be successful as we enter 2014 and beyond.

However, you can do better. The jump from a bare-bones website to a middle-of-the-road one is huge, no doubt. It's like going from a Burger King to an Outback Steakhouse.

It's the next step that makes all the difference, the one that jumps from a chain steakhouse — a perfectly serviceable chain steakhouse, but a chain steakhouse all the same — to a five-star restaurant.

That's the step to a website that's actually oriented toward converting visitors into clientele. A website that's designed, built, and maintained with the explicit goal of making your phone ring off the hook with new customers. This is one of the most powerful revenue generators in modern business.

And obtaining this goal is a lot easier than opening a five-star restaurant. (There's certainly no need to hire a fancy executive chef.) By employing a set of very basic tools, you can turn your website into this powerful revenue generator.

If you're going to have a website — and again, no matter what you do, you *need* a website — you might as well put it to work for you. That's what it's there for. If you're not maximizing its potential, you're leaving an incredible amount of money on the table. Don't let that happen. Get your website to not only attract visitors, but convert them into customers for life.

Designing your website for conversions

Here's the first thing to understand: No visitor will convert to a paying customer until your site has proven itself to the visitor. Every element of the site must underline your professionalism and credibility. It must say to the visitor: *We're the pros. There's no need to shop around; we are the solution to your problem.*

That's why someone's visiting your site, right? Someone needs to solve a problem. In your case, specifically, someone needs you to install, replace, or repair a roof.

If you can convince the visitor that you're the right person for the job right there, you've removed any need for the visitor to leave and keep checking around. *The visitor wants you to be the solution.* You just have to make it happen.

Only after you have proven yourself to your visitors can you focus on converting visitors to paying customers.

Open with a headline that sells: You might think your roofing business's name in a big font is all you need for your website. It's not. It needs to be on there, no doubt, but you want a headline that encourages your visitor to take action in some way. This is true for individual pages on your site as well — any place where you're selling a product or service needs a headline.

The great thing about a website is how easy (relatively) it is to customize. If your headline isn't getting the job done, it takes just a few clicks to change. A key to knowing how effective it is: Check the **bounce rate** for those pages. That's the rate when people click out of, or "bounce" from, your website.

Visitation logs in Google analytics make it easy to see how many people immediately leave after clicking on the page (or exactly how long they stick around). You can't do that with a newspaper or magazine ad. Trying out different headlines and reviewing the bounce rates lets you know what copy is most effective in retaining visitor interest.

Reinforce your headline with a great testimonial: You have many satisfied customers, right? Ask a few to write a testimonial. Visitors want to know that real people have used your products or services and come away thrilled. You can include more testimonials elsewhere — devote an entire page to them if you like —

but use the best ones on all pages where you're trying to compel action from the visitor. If you can add before-and-after photos or videos of the installation, even better. Show your engaged visitor exactly how you can solve the problem and do it *right*.

Address your visitors personally: The personal touch is very important. Again, this is especially important for people who are inviting you into their home to renovate their most valuable asset. People want to know that you're a real person who is proud of your business. Put together some copy — or hire someone with copywriting experience, if need be — to tell your visitors who you are, what you do, and *how you can solve their problem.*

Never forget that your visitor has a problem that needs to be solved. That's your focus. Your goal is not to sell someone on something. It's to solve a problem. (They might sound similar, but there's a key difference: Put yourself in the visitor's shoes.) As with the headline, you can check your bounce rates to see how effective the personal address is and easily tweak it as needed.

Provide some facts about the problem the visitor needs to have addressed: Generally, people search for products online because they want to save money, save time, or make life more convenient. Your roofing business exists to address one or more of these issues. (Especially since "do-it-yourself" roofing can be a dangerous consideration.) So provide solid facts about those issues, reinforcing in the visitor the understanding that a problem needs to be solved.

Offer your solution: Here's where you explain how you can solve the problem — and why your business is the best option to do it.

Maybe your products are just plain better than those of the competition. Maybe your prices are better. Maybe it's your experience in the industry. Think about *why* you would do business with you over anyone else. It's like writing a resume or a cover letter when you want a job: The employer has a problem (a job opening) that needs filled, so you're explaining why you're the best person to solve that problem.

Just as in a resume, don't get too bogged down in details: Focus on the most important facts that sell your business on the visitor. Whenever possible, include as many *quantifiable* facts as you can.

Call to action: There are some other copy elements that can help reinforce your pitch, but they can vary depending on a number of factors, so let's cut to this integral aspect. You need to wrap up with a call to action.

That call to action might be soliciting the visitor to call your telephone number, preferably through a click on your website, which makes it convenient *and* trackable. It could be to click on your email address link (again, it must be clickable — *always* make it easy for the visitor, and it helps you track. It could be to fill out an information form. (Keep this short and sweet; that's what you'd want when you visit a site.)

Impress upon the visitor that you can get this problem solved, and the solution is just a phone call (or email) away.

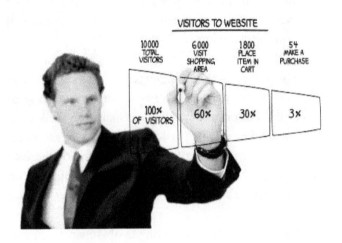

Improving your calls to action

The call to action (CTA) is one of the most important aspects of your website or landing page. You attracted a visitor to your site for one reason: to act in some way.

Everything on your site must be oriented toward converting that visitor, whatever that means to you: completing an online sale, gaining information on that customer as a lead, or simply making your phone ring. Here are a few ways to improve your calls to action:

Make sure your CTA stands out: You don't want anything on your site to be obnoxious, but make sure your CTA stands apart from the pack. Whatever your CTA is, make sure it really "pops" out. For text CTAs, use a different color for hyperlinks so it's clear to readers that the text is clickable and an action can be taken. For visual CTAs, use a color that starkly contrasts with the rest of your page.

Use strong, active language: This isn't the place to be passive or longwinded. Everything is funneling toward the visitor taking action, so make the CTA clear, simple, and direct. The visitor should understand exactly what he or she is getting and why acting on the CTA is the logical thing to do. If that isn't being clearly conveyed, make a change.

Be sure the value of acting is obvious: If you can't explain to a visitor why your offer is going to help in some way, why would the person click through? Your visitor came to the site to solve a problem related to roofing: The CTA needs to be the solution.

A brief overview of contact fields for landing pages and lead/customer generation

Your website's landing page has one absolute goal: Get customers, or at least get leads that you can convert into customers. The most integral part of making this happen is including a form in which your visitor can provide contact information.

That sounds like a simple enough affair, but how effective your lead generation is actually can depend heavily on how this form is designed. According to recent surveys, most marketers consider the lead-capture form to have a very significant impact on website performance.

You have a very short window of time to capture anyone's attention when that person visits your page — many experts put this window at a mere six seconds.

This rule is something to consider when designing your lead generation form. If the form seems too arduous or time-consuming to fill out, most visitors won't even bother.

The key is finding a balance between getting the information you need and keeping the form simple enough that it won't scare off your visitor.

A recent study indicated that the optimal number of fields to include in your form is *seven*. Whether that's the best for you depends on your site and your needs, but it's a pretty good number.

Include more, and you'll likely see a significant drop-off in conversions. Include less, and you're in danger of missing out on valuable information you might need.

Whatever you do, don't get into the double digits: That's as good as telling visitors you don't consider their time valuable. They're providing you information, not taking the SAT.

Contact Us

First Name *

Last Name

Phone *

Email *

Consultation Needs:

Security Code *

wdws9

Submit

Keep in mind that there's a big difference between what information you'd like to have and what you need to have. Name and email address are the two requirements, obviously. Depending on your type of business, you might ask for at least one phone number, zip code and/or and some other demographic information, such as household income or age range.

There are many other aspects to consider, but those are the basics. Ultimately, one of the best things you can do is review your landing page as if you were simply a visitor: Would you want to fill out that form? What advantage will you get from providing your contact info?

If your responses aren't overwhelmingly positive, you'll want to make some changes.

Grabbing your website visitor's attention right from the top

Visitors are great, right? Well, maybe not visitors to your home, at least when they're annoying in-laws or someone selling appliances door-to-door. But visitors to your roofing company website are great. If they're coming to your site, you're popular! You can check the analytics and see where they're coming from and what brought them there.

Of course… visiting the site is only half of the process, and you don't get any credit for half. A half-baked cake isn't something you want to eat. A half-vacuumed carpet just looks worse than a carpet that hasn't been vacuumed at all. You know what they say: close only counts in horseshoes.

It's great to have visitors, but it does you no good if your site can't convert those visitors into *customers*. It's like having the most-visited art gallery in town, but if no one ever buys a painting, you'll be the most popular artist begging for quarters on the street.

Your site can't just be focused on attracting visitors — it needs to *actively sell* those visitors on what you can exclusively provide them. It needs to get the point across right away.

How do you do that on your site? For one thing, figure out your top selling point to customers and try to make that the first thing they see. Your business's name is all well and good, but that alone doesn't sell the customer (unless your business is named Bill Gates' Free Money For Everybody Inc.).

Use that valuable real estate at the top of your site to sell your visitors on what you do better than anyone else. Figure out what they were looking for when they came to you — what problem they needed solved — and tell them clearly and directly why *you* are the best choice to solve it.

Whatever you do best, whatever your claim to fame, spell it out clearly and make sure visitors can't miss it. If that's the best price, the best guarantee, or whatever it is, *don't be shy about it.*

A note about SEO: As I noted earlier in this book, an integral aspect of ranking highly in search engine results is incorporating relevant keywords in your copy. These need to be in there, but far too many sites use keywords incorrectly. They stuff copy full of keywords to the point where the writing sounds like it's intended for the spiders (the search engine software that crawls the site), not for the visitor.

Never do this.

It will send visitors racing for the "exit."

A qualified Internet marketing expert can help you learn how to incorporate keywords so they sound natural in the copy.

Also, when keywords are used *too* often, this can actually *hurt* your SEO. Counterintuitive as it might seem, clunkily jamming in "roofing" or "roof installation " into every single paragraph works *against* you. The search engines will penalize your site in the rankings if the keywords appear too often, or not in the right places.

Yes, it's important to serve two masters, the human visitor and the search engine spiders, but always err on the side of writing intelligent, compelling copy for the visitor. Nothing will undermine your credibility faster than copy that makes little-to-no sense because it's only there to drive search engine rankings.

Conversion optimization factors

Let's go over some additional factors that help ensure conversions on your website:

Structure your navigation: On too many websites, the site navigation is cluttered and disorganized; it doesn't help drive potential customers to the pages that will give them the information they need. One of the biggest mistakes is creating site navigation that links to just about every page on the site.

When you provide so many options, it's confusing to the visitor, and you're not taking advantage of the opportunity to lead the visitor through a page-by-page process to deliver the message you want to convey. It's like suggesting a reader jump around randomly from chapter to chapter in a novel.

No matter your site's size, try to pare your navigation down to as few elements as possible. It's okay to have a dozen links or so in your navigation, but be sure they are *organized* in a way that helps visitors easily choose the right page.

Implementing structured navigation makes it much easier for visitors to quickly find the pages that are most interesting to them.

Give your site a voice: If your copy sounds like every other site, you're missing an opportunity to differentiate your business from the competition.

While the tone of your website's copy should always be professional, "professional" doesn't have to mean "boring." Too many people believe that business-oriented copy needs to read like the most academic of research papers. *This is a huge mistake.* Copy can be professional but still sound *lively* and *personal*.

Read through your copy and see if it sounds like you're simply having a casual conversation with a potential client. That's the kind of tone you want. The more personal flair you can inject in your website copy, the more it will stand out from the vanilla sound of so many other sites.

Having a unique voice gives you an edge. It tells customers you're different, and when they are choosing between you and a competitor, that might be the advantage that makes them choose your business.

Provide a box that lets visitors search your site: This depends on how well your site has been developed, but if you have good, useful copy on all your pages, a "search this site" feature can be a great boon.

If you're not sure how well your site delivers results when people search for certain common terms or phrases, test its functionality yourself before letting the feature go live. A search function that works poorly is worse than no search function at all.

If you do have a great site search that gives perfect results every time, this can help visitors find specific products, features, or information quickly without having to scan a bunch of pages.

This search data can also be helpful in telling you what people are looking for, allowing you to better promote those areas. Better promotion of your products and services means *more conversions*. Whatever options you offer in roof materials and services, make them easy to find.

Be consistent in formatting (fonts, bold, italics, images): There should be a consistent look and feel to all your pages, making them seem (as they are) all part of the same message.

While some homepages may look a bit different than the internal pages, it is important to be consistent from one page to the next. Your primary navigation should not change from one page to the next, nor should your footer, page layout, colors, etc.

When you don't have that kind of consistency, the onsite experience can be quite jarring, and this can ruin the experience for visitors. Any bad experience is bad for conversions.

Images and videos

The importance of images and videos in both conversions and overall SEO cannot be overstated. A site without visual elements is dry and hard to read, especially for people in this digital age. They are accustomed to seeing copy being broken up by images and videos.

Your leads will be looking for ways they can improve their homes both aesthetically and functionally, and a picture really is worth a thousand words. A video? It might well be worth a million.

Studies have shown that viewers are *64–85 percent more likely to buy* after watching a product video. Makes sense, right? Don't you want to know as much as possible about a product before spending your hard-earned cash?

As for images, they're essential: You might buy something relatively inexpensive without seeing a product video, but virtually no one buys without seeing an image. (Talk about buying "sight unseen!")

You sell products and services that can be clearly communicated through images and videos, so definitely incorporate them into your website. Anything that lets people see what they're getting and how a product or service works builds your credibility and the likelihood that you'll convert the visitor into a customer.

Even video testimonials can be a great way of turning visitors into customers. Seeing a real, live human being speaking exuberantly about what great work you do can go a long way with visitors.

Better yet, since few small businesses invest in these methods, adding images and videos is another great way to differentiate yourself from your competitors. They bring your business to life for the visitor, inspiring confidence in what you do.

Also, video just plain shows that you're real. You're not just some pretty website cooked up in the basement for a product or service that doesn't exist (or doesn't exist yet). It shows visitors that you're doing business on a day-to-day basis, accomplishing exactly what you promise in your website copy.

Delivering great conversion copy

I hit upon a number of content considerations earlier in this section, but let's talk a bit more about persuasive copy and how it can convert visitors into customers.

More isn't always better: Don't overload your pages with thousands of words of copy. You're trying to deliver a message, so provide just enough information to get that message across, and then get out of the way. You don't want to bury the visitor with minutiae that don't build your brand or deliver a conversion.

If you have a Frequently Asked Questions page, for example, resist the urge to pack it with tons of salesy language. Provide honest-to-goodness answers to actual likely questions.

For the most part, keep sentences and paragraphs short and to the point. Don't repeat information that you've covered elsewhere on the site. Your visitor's time is valuable, and digging through long stretches of copy to find necessary information will cause a visitor to look elsewhere.

But that doesn't mean to skip on content. Content really is king, and the more strong content you have on your site and your pages, the higher the traffic and conversions, generally. Content-rich sites also attract more links, which is always a good thing (presuming the links are legitimate and relevant). Be sure to have plenty of content; just make sure that the content you have is broken up into clear, concise, easily digestible chunks.

Show that you're trustworthy: Why don't people convert even though a site clearly shows that it can provide a definite solution to the visitor's need? Usually, the biggest roadblock is that the site hasn't sufficiently communicated its trustworthiness to the visitor. I'm sure it's rare that you get a client who picked a name out of a hat for something as important as home renovation.

Because far too many bad businesspeople have promised too much and delivered too little in the digital age, online customers tend to have their shields up.

They're afraid of wasting money, wasting time, putting their money on the wrong horse.

Your copy should be consistently focused on putting a potential customer's mind at ease. A money-back guarantee can help with this. Testimonials (both written and especially in video, as noted earlier) can help with this.

The visitor wants to believe you. The visitor wants to get the benefit from what you have to offer. As the business owner, you have to conquer that concern in the visitor's mind that you might not be legitimate.

Trustworthiness, transparency, credible authority, lots of high-value content, and plain old decency: These are your best weapons.

Everything on your site needs to show that you can be trusted. Provide real contact information. Display your photograph. If you're a Better Business Bureau member, make note of that (and display the seal).

Check the readability of your copy on various browsers, including mobile browsers: Nothing will run off a visitor faster than a website that's hard to read. The fonts and colors you use might look wonderful in Google Chrome but awful in Firefox. Test the readability of your site in all types of browsers and select options that display clearly (and in a compelling way) across the board.

While SEO is important, always put the human visitor first: I made note of this earlier, but it's so important that it bears repeating: If your copy reads like it's intended for search engine spiders and not the reader, *you're not going to convert*. This practice massively undermines your credibility and serves to confuse the reader. Get your keywords in there, but be certain that the copy in personable and conversational in tone.

Finding the balance in copy that's compelling for readers yet also keyword-rich is an art of its own, and a good Internet marketing expert and copywriter can be a great help with this.

Making it easy for buyers to check out online

By "check out," of course, I don't mean to check out mentally, or to check out of your site. I mean that if you use an e-commerce option on your site where people can use a checkout option to purchase immediately, you need to make it as easy as possible.

In your type of business, online checkout obviously is far less common than with companies selling products that can simply be shipped to an address.

However, given that you might have associated products that can be purchased online and delivered, I'll provide some more specifics about the process.

If this doesn't apply at all to your roofing business, feel free to skip ahead to the next main subsection, **"Onsite organic SEO."**

Now then, if by chance you *do* sell any products that can be purchased online:

You've sold the conversion — the visitor wants to buy from you, and buy from you now — so you want to place as few hurdles in the way as possible. It's an essential element of anything you do on the Internet: Give the visitor a reason to stay, to check out your other pages, and ultimately, to convert into a customer. If you use an online checkout system, keep the following points in mind:

Don't require registration/login: Sure, you want to get this information for lead generation and research, but it's not a barrier you want to put up when you need someone to convert.

When someone is on the hook and wanting to purchase your product, that visitor doesn't want to go through several more minutes of inputting info. Provide a guest checkout option to be sure to get the sale.

If you want to increase the likelihood of getting a full registration later, include a link in the confirmation email — with a discount on the next purchase simply for registering.

Let shoppers save their personal info: Why do people buy so much stuff on Amazon? It certainly helps that they have their shipping and billing addresses, along with their credit card information, already saved.

Amazon's one-click buying option isn't just convenient for customers; it also makes it incredibly easy for Amazon to convert a visitor. Just make sure visitors verify their billing with a security code each time.

Keep things concise: The tiniest things can prompt a visitor to duck out on a potential purchase at the last minute. The fewer fields you require a visitor to fill out, the better. Only ask for information you absolutely need, and offer shortcuts for shoppers like providing a checkbox that lets them indicate their shipping and billing address are the same.

Onsite organic SEO

Effective SEO isn't simply a matter of getting your site to rank as highly as possible in SERPs or driving as much traffic as possible to your site. You want people coming to your site who want you to install or repair their roofs. If the visitors who arrive aren't interested in roof installation or repair, they're obviously not going to convert into customers.

Effective SEO brings the *right* people to your site, people who are likely to convert. To achieve this, you want to use relevant keyword phrases not only in the copy people read, but also in the coding of the site itself.

This requires making use of **meta tags**, which help inform the search engines of what your site is all about. Of course, appropriate use of meta tags also gives your SEO a big overall boost. Search engines are better able to index these pages, providing a big increase in visibility and rankings.

Meta tags are HTML tags you place on the coding of the page. They can include **title tags**, **description**

meta tags, **heading tags** and **image tags**, among others.

Certain types of site software provide toolkits that make it easier to add these tags to your site without messing around with HTML — the most basic website programming language.

Title tags: These are extremely important indicators that inform search engines what your page is about. Things to keep in mind:

The title tag is not to be confused with your page heading. It belongs to your meta data and is the title users see at the very top of your web browser.

Page titles must be 60 characters or less. Because you have a limited number of characters, your title is precious real estate. Think like a user and type in search terms you know the user will use.

Some users will only look at titles, so your title needs to be something that will compel the user to click through when your result shows up in SERPs.

Titles for each page also must be unique; they cannot be repeated anywhere else on your site. The best SEO practice is to include your keyword in your page title, preferably at the beginning of the title. For your industry, as with all tags on your site, something specific to roofing should be incorporated.

Description meta tags: These describe what your page is about and are displayed along with your title in search results. Obviously, how your site is described will be a huge influence on whether a searcher clicks through to your site.

You are allowed 160 characters for a description tag. Make it something that's direct and compelling, and include words that users are likely to use to find the page.

Get your primary keywords in there, but avoid keyword-stuffing, and also try to include a call to action such as *read more about…, find out…*, or *learn all about…*.

An enticing description will increase your click-through rate. It also allows you to stand out from other sites that show up in SERPs.

Heading (H1) tags: These tags are intended to indicate the most prominent (and presumably most important) text on a page. These are followed by other H tags, H2 through H6, ordered from most important to least. These are important from an SEO perspective, but they also make the page easy to read.

Think about a magazine. Important things, such as the magazine's title or a front-page feature, would be in H1. A smaller article's title might be in H2 and a subtitle in H3. Google expects a webpage to be laid out with a series of headers that makes sense to the reader. These tell Google and other search engines what is most important.

It's important not to go overboard on H1 tags, just like you don't want to go overboard on things such as bold or italics. Emphasis is used to differentiate things as being more important; if everything is "important," then nothing is.

Abusing H1 tags will definitely get a webpage penalized by Google and Bing, so creating multiple H1 tags on a page purely for the purpose of trying to improve your search engine ranking is definitely frowned upon. It's generally best to stick with just one H1 tag per page.

Image tags: While both human visitors and search engine spiders can interpret words on a page, images themselves are (for the most part) only able to be interpreted by actual humans. To let the spiders know what's being seen in an image, you need to add image tags. These are also known as **alt-image tags**, because the text you include in them will be shown to your human visitors if the image fails to load for some reason.

Search engines crawl these tags as well, so by including your roofing-related keywords (when natural and appropriate) in these tags, you're once again improving your SEO for people who search for these keywords. As usual, don't stuff keywords into tags willy-nilly, because that can blow up in your face.

An additional way to improve image SEO is by giving the image's actual file a descriptive name. Instead of something like "IMG0097.jpg" for a particular type of roofing material, rename the file something like "Perma-lock-aluminum-green-sustainable-shingles.jpg." The hyphens allow search engines to recognize the composite parts as individual words.

Coupons

As more value-seeking people go online, the use of online coupons is rising exponentially. You've undoubtedly received emails from coupon/online deals sites such as Groupon, Living Social, Google Offers and more. As I noted earlier, coupon use helps incline people to try new products or services and — this is key — provide their *email addresses* and other contact information to the company offering the coupon.

Businesses often send consumers a coupon by email that they can print out and take to a store. Coupons are also appearing in banner ads, and of course, they're now showing up on mobile devices.

According to The Nielsen Company, 95 percent of shoppers like coupons and 60 percent actively seek them out. Since 2005, online coupon usage has grown 39 percent, according to Experian Simmons Research and Coupons, Inc.

According to Experian Simmons, more than 57 percent of online coupon users believe that businesses offering coupons care about keeping them as customers.

More than *70 percent* of online coupon users say they'd be willing to provide their email addresses and their first and last names to a business offering a coupon worth $2 or more.

Minimum Purchase $6,000.
Not Valid With Other Offers Or Prior Services.
Call or Email Us For More Details.

Minimum Purchase $500.00.
Not Valid With Other Offers Or Prior Services.
Call or Email Us For More Details.

Online coupons are effective at expanding a business's marketing area. They also help entice new customers who have been shopping at competitors' sites. Consumers will readily break with their routine shopping patterns to take advantage of a good coupon offer.

Coupons also often have a ripple effect. A customer who redeems a coupon for one particular product or service may consequently become sufficiently pleased with a business to also buy other products or services — at full price — down the line. Replacing one roof for a value-oriented customer might turn into a much larger renovation contract in the future.

Coupons also build online traffic. Consumers come to know that a business routinely offers coupons, so they keep returning to the business's website. The greater the traffic, the greater the SEO and the greater the potential for additional sales.

Online coupons are also highly measurable. They allow you to easily track which offers are attractive to visitors and which are not.

Section 3:

Customer Retention

CHAPTER 6
Customer Review Sites and
Reputation Management

The Internet allows you to tell everyone in the world how awesome your services and/or products are. You can go on about your incredible customer service on your website. You can develop advertisements that boast about your being the very roofer in your neighborhood, your city, your state.

And if that spiel is legitimate, worded well, and backed up by testimonials from happy customers, people will most likely accept that your assessment of your stellar reputation is genuine.

However, there's another side to dealing with reputation issues in the age of the Internet: You're not the only one who gets to weigh in on your business. Whether you like it or not, members of the general public will have their say on their experiences with your company.

As I touched upon earlier, customer review sites exist to aggregate information from people who have tried out a business and wish to write a review. While some people enjoy writing reviews of almost every establishment or service provider they interact with, most only take the time to write a review if they had a spectacular experience — or a truly horrible one. For this reason, businesses need to be ready to do a great job for every customer.

That's not a bad idea in theory: With your online reputation potentially at stake every day, you're presumably going to make a point of doing a great job with every customer interaction. That's extra impetus to go the extra mile, and it's better for the customers as well.

Of course, like anything else on the Internet, reviews can be gamed. As terrible as it sounds, some less scrupulous business owners try to artificially inflate their positive reviews by registering on these sites under a variety of different names. Even worse, these business owners often pan their local competitors — whether the pans are deserved or not — under other names.

Also, unfair reviews are sometimes posted by people who don't necessarily have a stake in the businesses. Some people just get a kick out of ripping companies — again, regardless of whether such criticism is actually warranted. Others try to trade super-positive reviews for free stuff, discounts, upgrades, and other perks. All of these underhanded strategies can influence the legitimacy of online reviews.

Because of this, most of the major review sites, along with Google, which includes online reviews as an aspect of its Google+ Local platform, set up algorithms that are intended to seek out and hide or remove reviews that are false or illegitimate. These algorithms have had mixed results, but they've at least applied some controls to a process that can be fraught with misbehavior.

The major sites also include some options to allow businesses to contest unfair or inappropriate reviews, and all allow the business to comment on reviews that appear, providing the company an opportunity to place the criticism in context and (if desired) to communicate a desire to address any legitimate concerns that were noted.

I'll talk about some of those options in a bit, but what's most important to take from this is that *you must be vigilant in reviewing your business's online reputation.*

This means paying attention to whatever people are saying about your business on review sites, in blogs, in news reports, and anywhere else. People who contract for something like roof renovation and repair are much more likely to post about the experience — whether positive or negative — than someone who simply bought a bagel from the coffee shop down the street. (Granted, there are people who do this, and we wish them all the best.)

If a reviewer hits you with a particularly negative review, it's *critical* that you not let it sit out there without any comment or response. If several bad reviews go unanswered, that can be extraordinarily damaging to your reputation.

Remember at the start of this book when I explained how more and more people every day are getting information about local businesses from their smartphones and tablets?

These devices make it unbelievably easy to quickly check out reviews when a potential customer pulls up your Google+ Local listing or a Yelp or Foursquare app. Bing has also integrated Yelp reviews into its searches.

These days, when someone simply clicks on your business in a maps application or does a search for nearby businesses and comes across yours, those reviews are sitting right there to be read.

No matter how well you promote your business, if several negative reviews pop up any time someone check you out, your business is in big trouble.

You absolutely can't afford to ignore online customer reviews. Good ones can be incredibly helpful, but bad ones can be devastating.

While there are lots of review sites online — some of which exist only to cover particular types of businesses or niches — here are the main players:

<u>Yelp</u>

This is the big daddy (or big mommy, take your pick) of review sites. As one of the first sites to marry local search, user reviews, and social networking aspects, it's grown astronomically since its founding in 2004, and its reach has expanded with ridiculous speed in recent years. As of January 2013, Yelp had more than 100 million unique visitors, an increase of almost 30 million from the same time the previous year.

Yelp also has a reputation system that lets visitors see which contributing users are the most popular, respected, and prolific. This can help visitors judge how legitimate reviews from these users tend to be, among other things. Business owners can also communicate with contributors who post reviews on their page through messages or public comments.

Having reviews of your roofing business on Yelp — especially positive reviews — is quite a boon. That's been true since the site launched, but it's especially true now. Yelp shares jumped 25 percent in 2012 after the ratings service reported that its base of local advertisers more than doubled and an increasing number of users took advantage of its mobile sites.

As mentioned earlier, the idea of a review aggregation site compiling plaudits and criticisms of various businesses is a controversial one. Some business owners have questioned Yelp's own credibility, especially after allegations emerged that some Yelp salespeople might have offered to hide negative reviews of businesses that paid for advertising sponsorship contracts.

Yelp has refuted these allegations, but they're pervasive enough to be concerning.

Some businesses also question the effectiveness of what Yelp's review filter, which is intended to prevent and remove illegitimate reviews. In certain cases, the businesses claim, reviews that would seem to be clearly false show up next to "real" reviews. In others, honest-to-goodness legit reviews get snagged by the filter and are not displayed.

In the same way that Google won't disclose the specifics of its search ranking algorithms to prevent them from being gamed, Yelp won't disclose the specifics of its review filter algorithms. Several class-action lawsuits have been filed against Yelp by businesses that have had positive reviews removed but have been unable to get negative reviews similarly redressed.

The fundamental allegation in most of these suits is that Yelp is trying to force businesses to advertise (which is how Yelp makes its money). However, as of this writing, Yelp had successfully defended itself against such claims.

Advertising with Yelp: While the company continues to contend that advertising with Yelp won't affect the display of organically created user reviews (either positive or negative), it's safe to assume that advertising on Yelp can't hurt. At the very least, the company makes no bones about the fact that your Yelp page will be better promoted and get more visibility if you're an advertiser.

However, that increased visibility might not be worth the return on investment for most small businesses. Many marketing experts believe Yelp's paid ads currently cost far more than what you receive in return.

The numbers can get a little confusing if you're not familiar with **cost per impressions**, which is the model Yelp uses for the ads. Much like traditional advertising, an impression merely means that someone has *seen* your ad. You're paying for the ad regardless of whether someone clicks through to your site. **Cost per click**, by comparison, only costs you money if someone clicks through.

With Yelp ads, the cost per impression (CPM) is exponentially more expensive than it is with standard CPM advertising. It's also much harder to track how effective your advertising is when you can't get click-through numbers. Yelp is also requiring a one-year commitment for its most favorable rates, which aren't particularly low in the first place.

Google+ Local

I referred to Google+ Local (sometimes styled as "Google+ Local" with a space) earlier. It's not a review site per se, the way Yelp is. It's essentially a merging of Google's local business listings (formerly called Google Places) with its social networking initiative, Google+ (aka Google Plus).

(Yes, that's a lot of Google words to take in. I know. I'll try to keep it all as clear as possible.)

Here's what you need to know: When people find your roofing company on Google, whether that's through a basic organic search, pulling up your listing through Google Maps, seeing a recommendation from a friend through Google+ — pretty much anything related to Google — your Google+ Local listing will be prominently displayed.

(This is achieved through first having a Google+ Business listing, as noted earlier.)

That's why it's important that the information on your Google+ Local listing, which you can add to and edit (to a degree), is always up to date and accurate. However, customers can also create reviews of your business that appear on your listing, which is where the similarities to Yelp come into play.

Much like Yelp, Google+ Local uses a reviewer algorithm to ensure the display of the most legitimate reviews. However, it also uses a Zagat rating that deduces a number grade for your business based on those reviews. (Yelp averages ratings based on a five-star system) This number grade on a 30-point scale gives users a fast snapshot on how well your business has been reviewed.

Google has stepped back from the Zagat system a bit, having determined that the grading system was too complicated for many users. It now lets users simply rate businesses "Excellent," "Very good," "Good," or "Poor-Fair." However, those grades still are considered toward the Zagat number grade.

In a very real sense, this makes user reviews and the Zagat number for your business on Google even more important than your standing on Yelp. More people search Google than search Bing (which uses Yelp ratings), and with Google systems integrated by default into all Android-based devices — Android being the most popular smartphone OS — you want to have the best Zagat number possible on your Google+ Local listing.

Google wants to make a company's Plus page the hub for every aspect of what the company does online. This includes a vast range of considerations, including business listing management, events, PPC advertising, integrated online payment, customer service, product delivery, buyer loyalty rewards, online deals/coupons, analytics, and much more. That makes it something you can't afford to ignore.

Google provides an option to flag reviews as inappropriate if they violate its guidelines, but as with Yelp, it can be hard to simply have a negative review removed if it falls within the guidelines. You can respond to a negative review with comments to provide your side of the issue.

As with Yelp, the more positive reviews you have, the better your average rating will be. Also, the more reviews you have in total (whether positive or negative) provides a great SEO boon, as that boosts your rankings in local search.

Foursquare

As with Google+ Local, Foursquare isn't a review site first and foremost. The platform was created to merge local search functionality with social aspects such as check-ins and tips. It's really a location-based mobile social networking platform, something I'll touch upon more in a bit.

The ratings aspect is actually fairly new to Foursquare. In November 2012, Foursquare added a number that rates a location on a 10-point scale based on the tips, dislikes, loyalty, local expertise, and popularity of all check-ins in a location's history. With more than 25 million Foursquare users, that's a lot of history to work with.

Also quite recently, Foursquare added the ability to link your Facebook account to Foursquare. This allows the activity of Facebook friends to help refine users' results, adding to Foursquare's functionality.

In another fresh initiative, Foursquare departed (slightly) from its all-mobile identity and rolled out a desktop homepage to target people who are not yet members. The idea is to keep pushing Foursquare as a Yelp alternative, bring people into the fold, and present its member reviews of businesses to a wide audience.

Also, Foursquare has joined Yelp in adding integration of the popular OpenTable reservation service, letting people place reservations directly through the app.

Foursquare isn't really the type of review/check-in site that aligns to a business, but it's something you should be aware of. Some people check in everywhere they go, and if your business has a roofing Foursquare listing, how you're reviewed there can affect your reputation and SEO.

Angie's List: pros and cons of advertising on this membership referral site

It might seem like Angie's List is a fairly recent phenomenon, but in reality, it's been growing slowly but steadily over the years. Its original offline incarnation began back in 1995 in Columbus, Ohio, and it expanded to the Internet (and national listings, as opposed to its original all-local focus) in 1999.

You've probably heard of Angie's List, because it's the type of review site that *does* align to services such as roof repair and renovation.

If you haven't heard of it, the idea is pretty simple: It acts as a review/recommendation site for various contractors, businesses, and services. In that sense, it's like Yelp and similar review sites, but Angie's List has a more complex methodology, one that is likely to produce reviews that are more accurate because they're more clearly verifiable.

For example, Angie's List is a paid membership site. Only paid members can submit reviews, which helps the site's staff ensure that reviews are unbiased and fair.

(Angie's List says it currently has more than 1.5 million members and more than 550 categories of local

service providers. More than 40,000 reviews are posted
to the site each month.)

Angie's List also has stringent requirements for
businesses listed on the site. You can create a profile
for your business for free, but you supposedly cannot
pay to be listed or necessarily increase your ranking
purely through a paid sponsorship.

However, some businesses have claimed that when
Angie's List contacted them to verify a review submit-
ted by a member, they were left with the impression
that advertising with Angie's List would be critical to
receiving a competitive ranking on the site.

Angie's List advertising options: Angie's List
knows it has a winning pitch just in the demographics

of its members: Most are college graduates and have an average household income of $100,000, according to the site.

That's an impressively prequalified group to whom you can market your services. Most are homeowners ages 35–64, exactly the demographic you're looking to serve in your industry.

Angie's List offers a few options for advertising. There's traditional advertising that can be done on the site, in the company's monthly publication, or through the company's call center. (Angie's List claims that listed businesses that also advertise on the site, in general, receive more than 10 times the number of inquiries from members.)

There's also the Big Deal promotion, in which a business can offer a Groupon-like heavy discount on services for a short time to boost their brand and expand their client base.

Angie's List member experiences: How effective advertising on Angie's List can be is obviously affected by its member base and those members' experiences. While many Angie's List members have reported very good experiences with the services, it's not hard to find members who have been less impressed, or even openly criticize the service.

Most of the concerns expressed do not seem to be about the quality of the reviews themselves, though some critics have questioned how objective Angie's List can be when it's accepting advertising from businesses, and others have noted that a number of categories on the site are pretty sparse when it comes to reviews.

The biggest issues with the user experience seem to depend on how tolerant you are of Angie's List interactions. The company regularly sends out emails with offers from advertising businesses, which can be taken as spam by many individuals.

It also sends out occasional automated calls for feedback and to solicit member reviews. Some people understandably consider this far more intrusive than the occasional email.

In addition, some former members have complained that the only membership options are to pay for a full year or be locked into a monthly auto-renewal process that the service makes it tricky to cancel.

How does this affect you as a potential advertiser? Well, if Angie's List is sending out your ads in a fashion that members find annoying or even obnoxious, it's going to be hard for the members to divorce themselves from that connotation in their minds.

The site's credibility wasn't helped by a class-action suit recently filed on behalf of Angie's List members. The suit claims that Angie's List automatically renews membership fees at a higher rate than customers are led to believe, calling the practice a "systematic and repeated breach of its membership agreement."

If Angie's List continues to gain a poor online reputation in some places — which is obviously ironic for an online contractor reputation service — you might want to consider whether you want your roofing business linked to theirs in your customers' minds.

Angie's List Advertiser Experiences: As with member experiences, you'll find a broad variety of opinions on whether advertising on Angie's List has proved valuable for local businesses. Some claim great experiences, finding a pool of motivated buyers that easily converts interested parties into clientele.

Others claim the return on investment just hasn't been there, especially when you balance it with what many business owners consider fairly intrusive pushes by Angie's List customer reps. Ultimately, it appears that whether your advertising is largely successful for you or not, either way you'll have to be able to live with the hard sell from Angie's List.

Here are a few things to consider:

- **Is your service likely to get solid reviews in general?** There's little point to advertising on a review/referral site if members who see your ads and click through don't like what they see when they get there. If you're definitely at the top of your game — and your customers agree — it makes sense to raise your profile on a review/referral-based site.

- **Are you already getting regularly leads and conversions from your free listing on Angie's List?** Advertising might increase that to some degree, but you'll likely either be locked into a lengthy commitment or pay full freight to find out. Can your business afford that?

- **Is your current advertising/marketing already reaching the Angie's List demographic in your area?** With only so many marketing dollars at your disposal, you don't want your efforts to overlap unless there's very good reason for it.

There's no question that Angie's List has steadily become an influential force in local businesses and services, especially for something such as roofing, but how that's going to pan out in either the short or long term is very much in question.

There's no shortage of strong opinions on the service, ranging from extremely positive to just as negative. The recent news of the class-action suit is also a big red flag for a company that's built on the concept of promoting highly reputable businesses.

Overall, I think there's reason to be concerned about whether paying for Angie's List advertising is worth what you get in return, but there's also no question that for some businesses, it could be a valuable avenue to pursue.

Garnering more reviews

While negative reviews obviously are bad for your business, the best way to counter them typically is to solicit reviews from satisfied customers. They're obviously far more likely to rate your business positively, and as I noted before, the quantity of reviews your business receives will provide a huge boost to your rankings in local search results.

Like it or not, there's no way to get rid of online reviews. They're simply a reality of the times. So instead of fighting them, do your best to get the most great reviews you can. Ways to do this include:

Solicit reviews on your website: I mentioned before that Yelp, for example, would prefer that you simply let customers decide on their own whether to review you. This seems a bit too strict. As long as you're not providing an outright benefit for a positive review, you should remain on the side of the angels.

You can create a page on your site specifically intended for reviews, and that can have a simple form they can fill out. The easier you make it for the customer, the more likely you are to get a review — particularly a positive one.

Add a review request to invoices and receipts: While putting the request on a printed form isn't as user-friendly as other methods, because the customer will have to then go online to do the review, it's a good complementary option. Also, if you use digital invoices or receipts, those can include a link your customer can use to easily go straight to filling out a review.

Put it in an email: If you're not already using an email list to keep in contact with customers and advise them of deals and promotions, you should be. Again, including a simple link to your own review form or that on a popular platform (such as your Google+ Local page, Yelp, Foursquare, etc.) makes it easy for the customer. Just be sure you're being careful not to spam your customers with emails, which could very easily prompt *negative* reviews.

Simply ask directly: When you have a customer tell you he or she loved your product or service, certainly reply that you greatly appreciate it, but what would really be great is if that person could leave a review on your site. Provide a simple, memorable URL the person can use to get it done.

Put up a sign: Yes, something as simple and low-tech as hanging a sign in your business reading "Review Us on Yelp!" can go a long way. It's just like old-school comment card boxes. If you add a QR code to your sign, your customers can simply scan the code with a smartphone, taking them right to your Yelp listing.

Offer discounts to Yelp users: Again, it's important to clarify here that you never want to "buy" a good review, but offering a discount to Yelp users obviously increases the likelihood of being reviewed. Yelp lets you post discounts, coupons, and events for free. If "Yelpers" see a discount, they're encouraged to stop on in, and active Yelpers write reviews.

This is also good because Yelp treats reviews of your business from active Yelpers (those who review a bunch of places, not just yours) much more favorably than those who only review a couple of places. The latter tend to get caught in the aforementioned Yelp filter.

Monitoring and responding to positive and negative reviews

It's never fun having your work criticized, regardless of whether the feedback is fair. When it comes to an online review, the impact of a complaining customer is far heavier than that of a card in a customer feedback box. It can imperil your business now and in the future.

This is why it's so critical to stay on top of how your business is being reviewed online. Remember that *reviews are good* for your business in many ways, so you shouldn't just put your head in the sand or take actions to stay under the radar. You do a good job, and your customers know this. The key is to get them to make this known, as I discussed in the previous section.

One thing you absolutely must do is *monitor all reviews you receive*. It's not as hard as it sounds. In fact, there are services available that can help monitor all the major review sites and let you review them together, and your Internet marketing professional can help with this. If you don't know what's being said about you online, you're powerless to adapt to it.

While it's most important to respond (and respond *quickly*) to negative reviews, the importance of responding to positive reviews is often overlooked. When people take the time to say something nice about your company, they like to know that you've seen the review and appreciate it. Thanking them and promising to do a great job will go a long way toward retaining those customers *and* attracting new customers to your company.

Also, if the only reviews you respond to are the negative ones, that leaves a poor impression on everyone who sees that page. Thanking people for glowing reviews and responding positively to critical reviews will always paint you in the very best light.

Granted, it can be challenging at first to find a positive tone in replying to a negative review, but it's not too hard once you get used to it.

After a cooling-off period, respond privately to the reviewer: You don't always have to start off with a public comment. On Yelp, for example, you can reach out to the critical customer first through a private message. Perhaps the criticism resulted purely from a misunderstanding or miscommunication that can be worked out.

Whatever the case, give yourself a little time to let your emotions ebb. It's natural to be upset by a negative review, but resist the temptation to overreact.

Instead, take a deep breath and evaluate the customer's complaint. Determine what has been (or can still be) done to address the issue. Engage the customer with a short and positive private response — either through the online review platform or via email — that recognizes the customer's criticism and discusses ways to remedy the situation.

By trying taking the issue offline, you can prevent a potentially ugly back-and-forth discussion that could draw even more unwanted attention to the review. If successful in resolving the issue offline, you can politely ask the customer to revise the review to note that the complaint was addressed or even delete it altogether.

If that doesn't help, provide a public reply: Even if you work things out privately, the reviewer might not elect to revise or remove the original negative review. Don't badger the reviewer; this might only lead the reviewer to further criticize your company on a follow-up comment or another review.

If you believe the issue was resolved, note that you reached out and successfully addressed the customer's concern. You might also include what steps you took to ensure satisfaction — for example, that a discount was offered or a replacement product provided.

If you believe there were legitimate inaccuracies with claims made in the review, offer a short response that corrects the facts. Again, keep it positive and professional. Maintaining the high road and appearing conciliatory to customer concerns is more important than establishing "your side."

Another thing to consider is that you should do everything in your power to discourage negative reviews in the first place (while encouraging positive ones). The foundation of this is simple: Do great work, provide great customer service, and generally make everyone who works with you feel happy and satisfied.

However, no matter how well your business is run, there will always be customers who are unhappy with the product or service provided. That's just the nature of business and the broad spectrum by which people interpret their customer experience. Some people are easy to please; others never seem to be satisfied. Two people could have the exact same experience and interpret it two completely different ways.

Customers who are unsatisfied often turn to online review sites to voice their frustration. Some wish to warn potential customers about your practices, some want to damage your company's reputation out of spite, and some hope to receive a response that could include an invitation to revisit the work or provide a discount or refund.

Many times, the customer will note concerns directly with a business before choosing to post them publicly. It's critical to seize this opportunity while you still have a chance to allay these concerns. Respond quickly and work out a resolution before a negative review is posted.

In most instances, staying positive, reassuring the customer that concerns will be addressed, and reaching some sort of compromise — even if that requires a rebate, refund, or other concession — is far preferable to the negative word of mouth a negative online review can generate.

Over time, these reviews can cost you much more than what would be involved in proactively remedying a customer's complaint.

CHAPTER 7
Check-ins for location-based services

Because several types of social networking platforms have a variety of aspects, they fall into numerous categories.

The names you see here won't be different from those I've discussed in recent chapters — specifically Facebook, Yelp, and Foursquare — but I'll be talking specifically about how these networks use check-in functionality for location-based services.

The ability to let users check in wherever they go is an increasingly potent aspect of social media and location-based marketing.

Location-based services are incredibly powerful tools for local businesses in this digital age. Foursquare, Yelp, and Facebook all provide some form of a location-based service (LBS), which uses the geographical position of a mobile device.

As more and more people use smartphones and tablets with GPS functionality, the base of location-based services users continues to rapidly expand.

When people check in at your business, you're provided all sorts of useful demographic information — who these people are, when they visit your business, how often they visit, whether they're visiting with others, and so on.

Check-ins are the foundation of location-based marketing. You get someone to check in to your location and give them a reason to spend money with you.

Similar to checking in to a hotel or flight, a check-in is a declaration that "I am here." Check-ins also allow you to track who is at your location at a given point in time.

Check-ins can either be active, in which a person physically chooses to use a phone or device to check in, or passive, in which a related action (such as swiping a loyalty card or filling out a registration checks the person in on its own.

Because your type of business is one in which most of the "work" will be done in your client's home, not at your business, check-ins will be less applicable to you, but they can play a role on occasion.

Geotargeting: A particularly interesting area of LBS is the addition of **geotargeting** — delivering messages and offers based on location — as a part of advertising.

This means that a smartphone user, for example, can automatically receive directed information based simply upon where he or she is physically located at a particular time.

Vacationing in Key West? Location-based offers and ads can appear on a user's phone purely determined on GPS coordinates.

A related aspect of geotargeting is **day-parting**, which lets businesses deliver time-sensitive ads, such as happy-hour deals at the end of the business day, or breakfast specials in the morning, and demographic targeting. Customers can use location-based services to take advantage of these deals.

Facebook

Facebook's first major push into location sharing was referred to as Facebook Places. That initiative didn't last too long, but the basic idea remains: Compel users to share where they are, connect with friends, and find local deals.

As of this writing, Facebook was in the process of launching its own geotargeting service to run on smartphones, similar to Google's Latitude and Apple's Find My Friends feature. This feature would tailor ads to customers based on their current whereabouts and daily habits.

Facebook has also been working on functionality that will help businesses where people regularly check in on the network rank higher in Facebook Graph Search results — another good reason to push users to check in at your business.

Because Facebook is such an incredibly popular social network, user check-ins also provide great free promotion for your business.

While this will vary depending on a user's privacy settings, generally whenever someone checks in at a business, that information is displayed on the person's timeline and is shared with all of that person's Facebook friends.

Foursquare

Still by far the most popular of all LBS platforms, Foursquare features check-ins, tips, badges, and points for accomplishments.

A leaderboard system prompts users to check in regularly, and Foursquare has the most comprehensive specials platform, a way for users to explore nearby tips, and an application programming interface (API) that allows anyone to use its functionality to write their own applications.

As I mentioned in the previous chapter, Foursquare has expanded into offering a desktop interface for local search that can be accessed by nonmembers, increasing its influence.

As with other location-based services, Foursquare also makes it easy for users to share their check-ins on social networks such as Twitter and Facebook, all of which can be beneficial for increasing brand awareness and SEO.

Businesses can easily encourage check-ins and re-ward return business by incentivizing people who check in regularly. The user who checks in most often at a business within a certain time period gets the "Mayor" badge, and other badges can be won by regu-larly checking in and providing tips.

Many businesses offer a perk to the Mayor and oth-er badge winners. Other businesses give something to first check-ins, for a certain number of check-ins, and so on.

Yelp

Yelp obviously is best known for its reviews, but check-ins have become increasingly incorporated in its user experience and benefits for business marketing campaigns.

Yelp's check-in offers and Yelp Deals allow users to search exclusively for businesses offering a Yelp Deal or check-in offer on the mobile Yelp app.

When a consumer clicks to view your full business listing, deals and offers will appear prominently at the top of your Yelp listing. This not only helps you gain additional exposure in customized searches, but it also can compel Yelp users to patronize your business.

Check-in deals and offers essentially act as coupons, and they can be used by service-based businesses to promote particular time-based discount opportunities, such as happy hours, to generate business during typically slow periods of the business day.

Those are just the biggest players, but there are many other location-based services with various levels of social reach and impact. The services are almost without exception free, and depending on how much time you have to invest in these services (and your particular type of business), they can provide a solid return on investment.

Using LBSs for Customer Engagement

Location-based services identify people who are enthusiastic enough to report that they're patronizing your business. Through LBS dashboards, you can identify your prospects and customers and engage them in an ongoing dialogue.

When you engage with someone, you're often creating brand loyalty. Think of engagement as the number of touch points you have with a group of people you care about, and then think about the quality of those engagements and whether they get you closer to your desired objective. LBSs also help build loyalty for your brand.

CHAPTER 8
Email Marketing

Think about the most tech-wary person you know, a true technophobe through and through. Can you think of anyone? Someone who has truly let the digital revolution pass him by. Doesn't have a mobile phone, much less the two (or even three) many people carry today. Doesn't have a laptop, much less a tablet. Has no interest in Twitter, doesn't care about Facebook, wouldn't know Yelp from yogurt.

At the very least, your friend almost certainly has a home PC and uses email.

In reality, almost everyone in America uses email and checks it regularly. Even people who rarely leave home check their email on a constant basis. Most modern email systems provide pop-ups and alerts to let you know you have a new email. Preschoolers have it. Great-grandmothers have it. With postal rates continuing to rise all the time, people continue to shift from communicating by snail mail to email.

And even if you don't own or use a smartphone, it's a fair bet your mobile phone — even one manufactured a decade or more ago — has the capability to receive and send email. Your email provider is most likely free to use, making it all the more valuable. Email access is easy, it's free, it's omnipresent.

Of course, email also produces a lot of spam, which is another thing entirely, but I'll get back to that.

Email marketing can be tricky in some ways, but it's a marketing initiative no business can afford to ignore. You have a free way to communicate with your customers and prospective customers who opt-in to your emails.

Can emails sometimes get lost in the morass of communications people get in their inboxes every day? Sure, but no less than direct mail advertising gets lost in the stack of junk that piles up in the mailbox. And direct mail costs *money*.

Email is by far the most cost-effective way to deliver marketing messages for your roofing business. You can send personalized, targeted, and interest-specific messages to a large number of people.

But there are other advantages. You can include links in email that prompt the recipient to click through directly to your site/landing page. Also, studies show that more than 80 percent of the email you send is opened in the first 48 hours after delivery, so you can get a fairly immediate response or action based on it.

First, avoid spam

Before getting into some email strategies, let me repeat something I touched on earlier:

Never spam.

Never, *ever* spam.

If you're sending out a mass email you think *might* be spam, it's almost certainly spam. Don't send it.

Sending out unsolicited emails is the very best way to get your business identified as a spammer, ensuring your emails a permanent grave in the ever-more-sensitive spam filters developed by Gmail, Yahoo mail, Hotmail/Outlook, etc.

When was the last time you even *checked* your spam filter, much less actually clicked on something you didn't recognize in it?

Spam emails are typically automatically deleted every 30 days or so for good reason: They're not beneficial, and no one wants them.

Even if your unsolicited email sneaks around the filter and reaches a recipient's inbox, most email providers provide a one-click method to report an email as spam. If your email looks spammy, you can expect this to happen.

Oh, and one other thing: *spamming is technically illegal*. So there's that.

Sticking with professional email standards keeps your emails legally compliant and ensures great relationships with the people who receive your emails.

An Internet marketing professional can help you understand all the ways your email could be classified as spam, though they mostly fall under common sense. Even if you always send emails to people who have opted in, there are two critical things to consider:

To send commercial emails that don't violate the law, every email should include two things: the *physical address* associated with your business (a P.O. box is accepted as long as it's associated with your business's actual location), and an *unsubscribe option*.

The unsubscribe process also has to be accomplishable by replying to a single email or by visiting a single web page, and you're required by law to remove anyone who unsubscribes from your email list permanently within 10 days of the unsubscribe request. You can't add that person back without the recipient's explicit permission.

Getting permission

If you haven't received permission from a recipient, your email almost certainly will be considered spam. So always get permission.

Technically, there are two types of permission: **implicit** or **explicit**.

Implicit permission occurs when someone shares his or her email address with you for some reason, such as filling out a contact form on your website for more information regarding a particular service or item.

That's opened the door for you to contact the person for that reason, but you haven't actually asked permission to continue to contact the person down the line with product offers and the like (unless that's clearly noted when the person signs on).

It's much safer to get explicit permission: Tell the person what to expect when by providing an email. If you plan to send promotions and other communications, be straight about it.

Once you've compiled your list (more on that in a moment), don't share it, don't sell it, don't trade it. Those are surefire ways to destroy your reputation with your customers.

Do I really have to be that careful? In a word, yes. As few as two spam complaints per 1,000 customers can prompt Internet service providers to block you from sending emails to their customers.

Even when you've received explicit permission, your emails can be interpreted as spam depending on how they're constructed or how often you send them.

In a sense, it doesn't matter whether the recipient asked you to email in the first place. If the emails appear too frequently, don't appear legitimate, or don't provide useful information, they can soon be interpreted to be spam.

Putting your list together

It's harder these days to compile a large list than it used to be, which is understandable: People are more careful about giving out their email address for fear of getting crushed by communications every day. Ever overlook an important email because it was buried in a bunch of inbox chaff? It's not a fun feeling.

In reality, you don't need a huge list for your email marketing to be effective. The best lists contain the names of loyal repeat customers, referral sources who respect others' privacy, and interested prospects who know you and your business well enough to recognize (and want) your communications. Ultimately, *quality* is much more important than *quantity*.

Unless your list is going to be extremely short, it's best to use some sort of database (or software specifically designed to organize emails and contacts).

In a roofing business, you want to establish great relationships with your customers, because repeat business can be a healthy proportion of your revenue. So you no doubt have some sort of customer database.

The database for your email list can be part of a customer database you currently use, or it can be something entirely separate. That said, it's *critical* not to get confused about which customers (and prospective customers) have agreed to receive emails from you.

A contact form on your website is one of the most common ways to compile an email list. If you're having trouble getting visitors to fill out the form, some incentives can help: *Join our email list and receive 20 percent off your first purchase.*

Design a great email

An effective email starts with the header. This includes the "From" line and address and the subject line.

The "From" line doesn't simply have to be your email address per se. You can set this up to read as your full name, or your company name, or both.

If another name (such as your website domain) might be more recognizable to people who have signed up for your emails, it's best to use this name. You don't want recipients to be confused about who's sending them emails.

The **subject line** is incredibly important, because this is the most information that will be provided before someone opens your email. It must compel the recipient to want to know more.

Subject line real estate is valuable, because most email providers only display the first 30 to 50 characters, and most mobile devices only show the first 20 to 30 characters. You need to get your point across concisely.

Add a sense of urgency to your subject line to increase viewer openings. Instead of *Free seminar on home renovation tips*, try *Last chance to register*. Make the recipient believe (but only when it's legitimate) that there's great benefit in acting immediately.

As with any professional communication, it's critical to spell words in your subject lines correctly and avoid spammy elements such as excessive punctuations (especially exclamation points), all-caps, capitalizing the first letter of every word, or using "Re:" (when it's not actually in response to anything). Also, ambiguous or deceptive subject lines such as "Hi!" or "I've missed you" are always to be avoided.

Be sure to brand your emails with a consistent template or a consistent color scheme. Including your company's logo also is a must. It should look like what it is: a professional communication from a professional business.

Visual elements: Marketing pros will tell you there are a lot of psychological elements you can use in your design to draw the eye where you want it to be. That's absolutely true, but it's beyond the scope of this book.

You should know the basics: Be sure the email is clear and easy to read. Be sure the most important aspects (particularly the call to action) are eye-catching and direct. Add visual anchors such as images (within reason) to break up the copy and make it appealing to read.

(Note on images: Without getting too technical, it's much better for your images to be referenced to a remote folder than embedded. Emails with embedded links are much more likely to be filtered as junk. A marketing expert can help you understand the difference.)

Content of your email

Be personable: As with your landing page copy, you don't want to sound too academic. Talk to your recipient the same way you'd talk to a visitor to your store or a client at a business meeting. Be professional, but don't be stuffy. You want to contract with this person for sales and/or installation, and you're explaining why it will be beneficial to that person. Do so in an informal, friendly way.

Links: If you're not linking to your landing page or a page that's specific to your offer in your email, you're wasting a great opportunity. Even if your email is purely communicative, there's no reason not to provide a one-click opportunity to get more information on you and your business in the body of the email.

If you're offering a deal on a particular roofing service or specific roof materials, hyperlink from the product in the email directly to the page where the product or service (and/or more details on the deal) can be viewed.

Use incentives and coupons: Every time you send an email, it should have a purpose. "Hey, I'm still here!" is not a purpose. (Even if that's what you're most looking to communicate.) Show your appreciation for people on your email list by offering them exclusive promotions and discounts. Give them the opportunity to act first on new products and services. They're opening up their email boxes to you, so reward them for that.

An informational email works well, too: Maybe you're not looking to promote a particular item or service at this time. That's fine. Is there some information or fresh news about the roofing industry that would be (truly) interesting to your customers? If so, that's enough reason for an email.

Don't waste people's time by sending these out constantly or for minor matters, but delivering useful information is a great way to stay in people's minds, along with a great excuse to include links to your website and continuing offers.

If you don't have the time or resources to create your own emails, there are lots of great copywriting services that can help you achieve your goals, and many are very reasonable.

Monitoring your email results

Again, I won't get into all the technical aspects here, but there are great services that will allow you to easily track your return on investment from business emails. They let you review lots of useful data, including:

- Which emails bounced
- Why they bounced
- Who opened the emails
- What links the recipient clicked
- Who unsubscribed

- Who forwarded your emails

This data can go a long way toward helping you refine your email marketing efforts and improving conversions.

There are more elements to successful email campaigns, but understanding these basics will help you determine the best way to use email to help your business succeed.

Email lists: Should you purchase them? (Spoiler alert: no.)

A precompiled email list sure sounds like a good deal when you're marketing your business. You have a list of emails for people who are prequalified to be interested in roof installation. What could go wrong?

Um... just *everything*.

The first thing to remember is that even if you worked with an email list provider for a list that has been shaped to include only customers who meet certain demographic or psychographic (personality, interests, lifestyles, etc.) standards, *it's not really an opt-in list*.

No one opted in for communications regarding your service or product. The people on that email list simply opted in to an email communication from someone at some point in time (like the list provider). When you're emailing people who haven't shown an interest in your business, that's something most people consider spamming — and you're not likely to see much return on those communications anyway.

Also, there's really no such thing as a good email list that's for sale. Typically, any addresses that once had value have since been spammed by a variety of other business.

Yes, there's that word again: **spam**. We're printing it in bold, even though we rarely do that (extra tip: use emphasis tools such as bold sparingly so they don't lose all meaning), because it's so important to understand that contacting people through a purchased email list almost always equates to spam.

If your business is defined as a spammer, your email deliverability and the reputation of your IP address almost certainly will be harmed. Organizations dedicated to combating email spam have a tool called a **honeypot**. It's a planted email address that, when emailed, identifies the sender as a spammer.

There are other spam traps that identify if an email address is old (or no longer valid) but still receives consistent traffic.

There are effective ways to build email lists through proper means. For the sake of your business and its reputation, don't go the purchased email route. The rewards are few and the risks are far too great.

Section 4:

Monitoring and

Measuring

CHAPTER 9
What Gets Measured Gets Done

Yes, "What gets measured gets done." It's a well-known saying, and properly so: it works. When you're constantly monitoring and measuring your results, you can determine what's working and what's not. You can find the places where you need to revise, tweak, or even go in an entirely new direction.

Here's the beautiful thing about today's digital world: Monitoring and measuring your marketing efforts is now incredibly fast, unbelievably precise, and unexpectedly easy.

Not only that, but you have far more flexibility now in what you do with the information you get from your analytics. You'll know what you need to do and be able to do exactly that on the fly.

You can make changes to your website that go live immediately. (Yes, it can take some time for spiders to crawl the site, but changes you make will be seen by human visitors right away.) You can revise a PPC ad so that leads see the new information the very same day. When your analytics show that your customers are excited about a particular product or promotion, you can showcase it on social media.

Google Analytics

This is the best known and most popular of the user-friendly measuring tools, owing at least in part to the fact that so many business use Google advertising and other services.

In essence, Google Analytics generates detailed statistics about a website's traffic and traffic sources, along with measuring conversions and sales. This makes it an incredibly useful tool for marketers and business owners. The basic service is free, but there's a premium option available for a fee.

The service can track visitors from a broad variety of sources, including search engines, social networks, direct visits, and referring sites. It also displays advertising, pay-per-click networks, email marketing, and digital collateral such as links within PDF documents.

Google Analytics is completely integrated with AdWords, making it easy to review online campaigns by tracking landing page quality and conversions. Target goals can include sales, lead generation, viewing a specific page, or downloading a particular file, among other options.

Some of the many things you can analyze

Whether you use Google Analytics or another site-monitoring tool — the former is practically a requirement, and other tools are best used in combination with Google Analytics — here are some of the many things you can monitor:

- **Number of visits**

- **Number of people who actually visited your site:** A person may visit your site more than once, and each time, that's a separate visit.

- **Number of pages per visit:** Each time a person visits your site, the visitor might view a single page or go on to view dozens of them. (If you've populated your site with great content, hopefully the visitor is checking out all of your great options in roof materials.) The greater the number of pages viewed per visit, the more people are actually exploring the information it contains.

- **List of most visited pages:** This indicates the number of visits received by each individual page. You can then use this list to analyze which themes, products, and information grab your customers' attention the most. It also includes your campaign landing pages, providing you with final statistics for each of your marketing initiatives.

- **Length of stay:** This indicates how long on average your visitors stayed on your site, thus indicating how well they relate to your content. The longer your visitors stay, the greater their interest. This gets to the issue of **bounce rate**, which I'll touch on in a moment.

- **Origin of visitors:** This identifies what site someone was viewing on the Internet immediately before visiting your site. Think of it like a flight: One city's airport is the place of departure; the other is the place of arrival. It's beneficial to know where your visitor arrived from — that makes it much easier to know what prompted them to check out your business.

- These origin statistics can show **direct visits**, in which customers enter your URL directly into the browser; **site referrals**, in which a visitor comes to your site after clicking on a link at another website, a **blog** or **social media network**; and **search engines results pages**.

Tracking phone calls

Businesses that mostly do e-commerce and sell products and services online aren't so concerned with phone calls. They do the vast majority of their business digitally.

In fact, many products are sold online without any direct involvement by the person selling them. An automated purchasing system is set up, the customer purchases the item, and it's automatically delivered digitally (if not a physical item) or goes into a queue to be delivered from a drop-shipper or wholesaler.

For a brick-and-mortar business such as yours, it's an entirely different story. While you might (and should) get inquiries by email or through a form on your website, many inquiries from leads will be coming in over the phone.

Sure, some hair salons have online registration systems, just like restaurants have online reservations (either on their own site or through an app such as Open Table) and many other service providers. But even as we enter 2014, when most people want to make an appointment with a local business, they call.

When someone wants something as substantial as home renovation, they want to establish a relationship and a feeling of trust in real time, either in a phone call or in person. (There's also Skype, videoconferencing and other types of real-time chat, but I'll stick with the basics here.) This is why understanding how to track phone calls that originate from your website is so important.

Many people now make phone calls simply by clicking on a link. When they do it on a desktop computer, typically they have it set up to call through Skype, Google Voice or some other VoIP (that stands for *voice over Internet Protocol*) service.

These days, however, many more people will be visiting your website — or Google+ Local or Business page, or your Yelp listing, or your Facebook Fan Page, a PPC ad, etc. — on a digital device that's *also* a phone.

Because your phone number is also a link that allows people to call you with a click, they can contact you *immediately* directly from your listing. The more you make it easier for the lead to contact you, the better. That's why having a *clickable* phone number (just like a clickable email address) everywhere you have a Web presence is so important.

When your phone number is clickable, an experienced Internet marketing pro can easily track phone calls made from your site and listings. You can see how many leads are coming directly from your site in the form of phone calls (emails also are easily tracked, as you might assume).

You can see what times of the day the site is most effective in getting phone leads, how long people visited the site before calling, what page they were viewing before they called, and so on. This allows you to optimize your site to convert the most traffic into leads.

Bounce rate and site engagement

As I indicated earlier, your website no longer can merely exist because "everybody has one." It's not just there to display a picture of your warehouse and some basic contact information.

Your website needs to be *actively engaging* its visitors. It must be designed to communicate trustworthiness, engage the visitor, sell the visitor that you're the best solution to a particular problem, and convert the visitor into a customer.

You can implement all the best practices toward creating an engaging, high-converting site, but only through analytics will you know how well it's working — and which aspects of the site are delivering the conversions (and which are not).

The first thing most experts focus on when assessing site engagement is the **bounce rate**. Though the definition for this can vary a bit, I'll stick with the Google Analytics definition: It's the percentage of visits in which the visitor only views *one page* before leaving the site.

For certain businesses, having a high bounce rate isn't a terrible thing; they might be trying to communicate something very simple with a very basic single landing page. They might not even have more than one page on the site.

However, a high bounce rate is very bad for a business in your industry. You're selling products and services that require time for the customer to research.

You want the visitor digging deeper into the site — at least as long as that's producing conversions for you.

Bounce rate can be broken down in many ways, including factoring which visitor origins have the highest bounce rate and which have the lowest.

The other concern regarding bounce rates relates to SEO: Google and other search engines take your bounce rate into account when ranking you. It's another key reason to design your site in a way that invites the visitor to stick around and check out additional content on your site.

Reducing bounce rate

If you've set up your site in a legitimate manner with white hat SEO, and at least some solid content spread across several pages, you don't have to worry about the worst bounce rate percentages.

Those terrible numbers typically are reserved for sites that attract visitors through misleading (black hat) means. They persuade people to click through to the site by implying there is a diamond in the stocking when they clicked through, but what they find is a lump of coal. The visitor immediately clicks out of the site, which is why bounce rate is such a major factor in search engine rankings.

Still, the better the bounce rate, the better for your business. Ways to improve your bounce rate include:

Browser/mobile compatibility: If your site isn't optimized for mobile devices, you'll get a lot of bounces from visitors trying to access it on phones. Also, be sure your site displays properly on all the major Web browsers.

Pay off your ads on your site: When someone reads an ad that promises one thing, but clicks through to discover another, that's a quick bounce. Be sure your site is set up logically and intuitively, and be sure your site delivers exactly what your ads promise.

Don't annoy the visitor: If you hit the visitor with pop-up ads, chat windows, a blatant call to action, and more right on the landing page, kiss that visitor good-bye. Keep your landing page attractive and welcoming. Let the visitor feel "at home" and interested in exploring before placing demands. It never hurts to think of a virtual visitor as a guest in your home.

Check your page load times: If your site uses extremely complicated design or lots of graphics, some pages could take awhile to load — this is a known factor in high bounce rates. You can test page load times through analytics. If your pages are taking substantially longer than average, it's time to do some redesign.

There are ways to streamline the mobile version of your site so that large files for videos of your products, for example, do not automatically display. The visitor can be provided an option to display these files if desired, which might be the case, for example, if the visitor is viewing the site on a tablet or large-display smartphone over Wi-Fi.

Improve your content: This is a general tip, but it's one of the most important. Small things such as spelling and grammatical errors can cause a visitor to lose faith in your business and bounce out. So can something that could be considered polarizing, such as political statement. High-quality content returns low bounce rates. Low-quality content returns high bounce rates.

The five basic traffic metrics

When analyzing your site's traffic, there are five basic metrics to understand:

Sessions: A session is another word for a single visit. It's one person visiting your site any one time. If someone visits your site 15 times, those visits count as 15 sessions, whether she stayed on the site for 5 minutes or 50.

Unique visitors: A unique visitor is one person visiting your site any number of times during a defined period. If someone visits your site eight times in a week, that person still counts as one unique visitor.

Page views: A single page view is any one visitor viewing one page of your site, one time. The page must have a unique address (URL). If someone visits your landing page and then clicks a link to your About Us page, those are two page views.

Time on site: This is the total amount of time one visitor spends on your site in the course of a single session. Average time on site is a critical measure of visit quality and visitor interest.

Referrers: If someone clicks a search result link to reach your site, the point of origin — the departure airport I talked about earlier — is known as the referrer.

There are many ways in which a marketing professional can use these metrics to help improve your site's traffic and conversions, but the details go somewhat beyond the scope of this book.

What's critical to understand regarding monitoring and measuring is the digital age allows you to precisely understand every aspect of your site's effectiveness and your marketing campaign — and it allows you to make virtually instantaneous changes to optimize your efforts.

Knowing which referrers tend to send the most traffic your way can help you decide where to focus your marketing and promotional efforts.

If most visitors are checking out particular types of roof materials, for example, and/or spending more time on those pages (enlarging the images, watching the videos, etc.), you'll know what those particular leads are most interested in buying.

Of course, it's just as important to know how well visitors are converting who arrive from particular referrers — another statistic that can be easily mined from the data.

Analytics essentially provide you honest feedback on all your efforts. People might tell you they like one thing or another, but the proof is in how long they spend on a page, what they choose to click on, whether they decide to move forward and convert to a customer. The digital age lets you see all that information in a way that can power your success.

Section 5:

Working with a

Marketing Professional

CHAPTER 10
Finding a Qualified, Principled (Internet) Marketing Professional

You know why I put Internet in parentheses: Because as I've noted several times before, Internet marketing *is* marketing as we enter 2014 and go forward.

However, many marketers remain behind the 8-ball when it comes to understanding how to promote their companies online.

You'll want to find a company that specializes in Web-based marketing, but it's just as important to be sure the company uses appropriate methods that will keep you on the good side of Google, other search engines, and laws regarding spam and legitimate marketing methods.

Using an Internet marketing pro vs. doing it yourself

In many ways, we now live in a DIY society, and that's a good thing. With the expansion of 24-7 Internet access into people's homes, we now have a wealth of information at our fingertips any time of day.

It's like having access to hundreds of thousands of libraries at all times, right there in your office, or living room, or porch, or wherever. You can take a tablet PC to the beach and access 100,000 times more information than a person could at the largest big-city library 25 years ago.

All of that information makes it much easier for people to solve their own problems. Need tips for changing the pedals on your bicycle? There are not only step-by-step guides on the Internet, but YouTube videos as well — and they're all completely free.

Some businesses take this approach for their Internet marketing efforts. While a few are successful at this, that's generally because the business is related to Internet marketing, or something closely affiliated with it, in the first place.

For most business owners, the best use of your time is doing what you do well. You replace and repair roofs. You know your inventory inside and out. You know what type of roofing makes the most sense, functionally and aesthetically, for a variety of homes. You know how to hire and manage a crew. You know how run a business and make a profit while satisfying your clients.

That's a lot on your plate. You should be repairing and replacing roofs, not trying to determine which keyword phrase gets you the best PPC results. You should be ensuring your latest roof installation went perfectly, not figuring out how to edit image tags in your website code to improve your search engine rankings.

The DIY route might make sense if employing the right Internet marketing firm were extremely expensive, but it's not. Some great firms are very affordable, and the increase in business will pay for the initiative many times over.

When it comes to justifying the cost, also consider this: Good Internet marketing can help you become more selective.

The more potential clients or customers you have, the choosier you can be. If you only have 10 clients (but can handle 25), you might have to undersell your services, because you can't risk losing the 10 clients you have. However, if you have 50 people who want to use your services, you can set your prices at a much more appropriate rate.

Red flags to watch out for when choosing an Internet marketing firm

Now that you know the benefits of hiring a professional to handle your Internet marketing, you need to know how to select one. The skills, experience, resources, and customer support abilities of various firms can vary widely from one to another.

Here I'll hit on "red flags" that are indicative of the way certain Internet marketing consultants, particularly those with large firms, do business. I'll follow that with a short explanation of how a legitimate business would handle the situation.

RED FLAG #1:
Conflicts of Interest

The problem with many large Internet marketing firms is that while they are managing your campaign, they are also managing your direct competitors' campaigns.

You and your competitors all are competing for presence on the first page of search engine results. The space is limited. Whose interest does the firm have in mind?

In addition, at a big firm, your account representative is hired to sell — not to manage your campaign. How can he manage your campaign if he's pressured by his managers to hit sales goals every week? The rep's incentive is to sell, not to generate more sales for you.

If he triples your sales, he doesn't benefit it any way. If fact, if he ignores your account, he actually makes more money. Your account gets neglected and performance suffers.

At a legit marketing firm, your dedicated account manager is a dedicated marketing engineer, not a salesperson. The managers are under no pressure to go out and find accounts. Their sole purpose is the continual optimization of your campaign, to bring in customers and make your phone ring.

They have top-level technical expertise in Internet marketing and have helped numerous businesses — in particular, roofing and other home repair/renovation businesses — just like yours transform leads from online to your phone line.

RED FLAG #2
Lack of transparency

Most companies doing great work want to illustrate what they can achieve. That means sharing all the numbers with their customers. However, many large Internet marketing firms do not provide you with all the data associated with your campaigns.

For example, they do not show you what exact keywords they bid on, which match type they use, what the bounce rate is, or the quality score associated with each keyword.

Those terms might be unfamiliar, but they're easily explained by a quality consultant. You don't need to know what all these words mean, but you do need to know that these are the words that measure whether a campaign is actually working.

A good Internet marketer will not shy away from providing you a result with all this information. When you do good work for a customer, you want to show it off. You want your customers to know exactly what you're achieving for them. When that information is hidden, you have no way to know.

It's equivalent to FedEx sharing its percentage rates for on-time arrivals. These are the key numbers that measure whether your marketing is succeeding or failing.

At a legit marketing firm, all the data is shared with you. The company should share with you exactly what it has done with your campaign every week. If a company does good work, why would it do anything else?

RED FLAG #3
Retention through contracts, not by results

A number of large Internet marketing firms require contracts with minimum term commitments. Why is that a concern? It relates to how Internet marketing works.

Business owners generally will know within 2–3 months whether their marketing provider is achieving the results they'd been promised. Unfortunately, if they want to terminate their campaign when they have a minimum term commitment, they're out of luck. Whether the campaign is soaring or nose-diving, the business owner is on the hook.

If you're providing real, quantifiable results every month, why require a minimum term?

At a legit marketing firm, programs run month to month. Most partners see results in 30 days, but sometimes it takes 2–3 months, depending on the particular market.

After that time frame, you can terminate the service if you like. However, after 90 days, customers typically are so thrilled with the results that they don't want to leave. They've achieved tremendous growth in their revenue and want to keep that going.

RED FLAG #4
Lack of technical knowledge

A lot of large Internet marketing firms do not actually employ Internet marketing experts. They employ salespeople.

When you sign on with these firms, the person managing your pay-per-click campaign is not a marketing pro. It's your account representative. Here's the problem: She's a salesperson, not a marketing technical engineer.

These account reps undergo a few weeks of crash training and are expected to manage your campaign. In fact, they are not certified. Internet marketing is very complicated process, and most salespeople are not good at it. They earn their pay by being good at sales, not Internet marketing.

At a legit marketing firm, your dedicated account manager is a dedicated marketing engineer, not a salesperson. The managers' sole purpose is to optimize your campaign and get new customers calling you.

Unlike larger companies that check in on your account once a week, a legit company will actively manage your account on a daily basis. It will monitor and adjust your campaign every day to achieve the outcome you and the expert decided upon together.

Once the firm has a great pay-per-click campaign set up for you, it can make sure it's always achieving results by working continuously to improve it.

Your target market's keywords might change every month. Your competition might suddenly be paying more for same keywords, lowering your ad position. Perhaps your competition comes up with an ad that has a better offer — your ads still show, but fewer people click on them.

Continuous management is essential to keeping your online advertising costs down. That's what a good firm does.

RED FLAG #5
Focusing on the number of ad clicks, rather than on your business

With many large Internet marketing firms, it's in their best interest to drive more clicks and spend all your budget each month, then come back to ask you to spend even more. The company makes its money based on the percentage of your spending.

If that sounds ridiculous to you, well, it does to me too. You're paying good money to drive customers to your website. It is critical that these visitors go on to call your business.

These companies do not do any website conversion optimization to ensure that traffic turns into customers. They only care about delivering traffic to your website, not to your phone line.

Here's the problem with that: If your website isn't optimized in the first place — if it has a hard-to-find phone number, no offer, etc. — no amount of traffic will save you. The primary purpose of the website is to create contact by phone or email. Optimizing your website for this purpose is a vital part of this process.

At a legit marketing firm, it all comes down to the bottom line: delivering a high return on investment. That means turning website visitors into sales. Conversion rate optimization is an ongoing process of testing and tuning your website to make your phone ring. A good firm teaches you how to fine-tune your site to convert more online visitors into sales.

Conclusions

Staying ahead in a digital world

I've covered a lot of information in this book, and I realize it's a lot to take in. Even without digging into all the minutiae of various marketing efforts in a digital world, as you can see, it's a very different battlefield than companies dealt with 10 years ago, even five.

I could tell you that everything will reach a nice, level plateau for a while, that once you understand how successful business marketing works in a digital world, that you'll be up on the status quo for the next several years.

But that isn't true.

The one constant of successful business marketing today is that nothing is constant. Social media networks that were incredibly influential a few years ago (I'm looking at you, MySpace — and you, Friendster) are virtually extinct today.

Mobile phones that were cutting-edge a few years ago can't handle the vast majority of applications that are most used today. Websites that attracted tons of traffic and converted visitors almost automatically are ineffectual today (if they haven't been updated since).

It all sounds scary, but in truth, the ever-changing influence of technology on local businesses in this digital age is a very *good* thing — for those willing to adapt and use it to their benefit.

These circumstances provide business owners who can adjust on the fly an enormous advantage over local competitors who are still doing business the 2005 way, much less the 2000 way.

I feel fortunate to have worked with lots of great small business owners, particularly several roofing company owners, just like you. I've seen firsthand how much more revenue they can generate by employing the very same tools I cover in this book.

These tools allow small business owners to separate themselves completely from the pack. They can attract and target prospective customers long before their competitors are even aware of them. They can evaluate and measure their marketing approaches on the fly and improve them with virtually no delay.

Yes, things move fast these days. No, it will never be as simple as it was to simply run a local business. But that's simply the reality. Times change, and people who accept that change and adapt to it will thrive. Those who do not, no matter how good they are at what they do, will stagnate and die off.

Perhaps that doesn't seem fair, and that's under-standable. If you're the best in your city at installing roofs, shouldn't that be all that matters? You do a great job at a fair price. All business should naturally flow to you.

In truth, that's never been the case. Simply being good at your chosen vocation might be enough if you're an employee, but you're not an employee. You're a business owner. You took the plunge to be enterprising and run your own roofing company, and that's wonderful. And as the owner, you know that whatever you do that running the business side is its own discipline, one that's very different than simply product sales and installation.

That discipline *has* changed well before now. It changed with the advent of websites and email. It changed when payroll went from being calculated with pencils and erasers to Excel spreadsheets. It changed when you went from contacting employees on pagers and walkie-talkies to mobile phones.

Things are just changing faster now. Much, much faster. And it's not just the speed of things — it's also how far their influence has spread demographically. Incredibly powerful technology is in the palm of people's hands, and they're using it. Every age, every race, everywhere.

It doesn't matter if you're in the heart of a big city or working in a small town. Your customers, and your potential customers, are employing this technology in their day-to-day lives, and it's only going to become more pervasive.

This doesn't mean you need to become a master of the digital world. You can run your roofing business and focus on what you do best. I've worked with lots of small business owners who just wanted the phone to ring. And that's what I do. I employ the techniques in this book, in addition to other methods, as necessary, to attract visitors, to convert those visitors into customers, to make a business's phone ring off the hook.

The business owner can be as involved or removed as he or she likes. Some proprietors want to know and help control every aspect of the process. We can do that. Some want to be almost entirely hands-off. We can do that too. And anything in between? Never a problem.

That's because you know best how to run your business. You know your strengths and weaknesses. You know what requires your direct supervision and what you can delegate. The same thing works with marketing in the digital world.

You can figure out what works best for you. A qualified marketing expert will adjust to your needs and expectations. The only important thing is making your phone ring.

Having read this book, you might think you need to employ all these marketing aspects immediately. On the other hand, it might sound so overwhelming, you might think it's best to ignore them altogether.

It should be obvious that the second option isn't an option at all. Other small businesses, particularly those in the roofing industry, are employing these initiatives. They are getting more bang for their buck, expanding their customer bases, and identifying the best and most profitable customers, using these methods.

That said, your business doesn't necessarily need to do everything that's listed here. It depends on what you do. It depends on your budget. It depends on what resources are best directed to provide you the very best return on your investment.

Various marketing companies do things different ways. My company offers a 100 percent money-back guarantee, because we know what we do works. We know how to attract people who are looking for exactly what you provide. Really, we're just like you: We're good at what we do, and we want to share our expertise with local businesses and help them grow.

Things move fast in the business marketing world, and I don't expect the proprietors I partner with to stay up on these things. That's the service I provide. I stay apprised of every twist and turn and use that knowledge to benefit my partners. That's what a good marketing expert should do. My partners stay ahead of the game, and it's a game that changes month to month, sometimes week to week.

Now that you've learned the basics of marketing in today's digital world, take some time to assess your marketing efforts and how they've been working for you.

Do you know how effective your advertising is?

Do you know what customers are saying about your roofing business online, in user reviews, in ratings, and on social media?

Do you know whether people can easily access your website on tablets and smartphones?

Do you know whether your company even shows up on Google Maps, on Foursquare, on Apple Maps?

If you don't know the answer to these questions off the top of your head, it's probably time to take a long look at how you're marketing your business in a digital age.

Business owners who know the answers to these questions are highly visible to potential customers. Those who don't are typically flying way under the radar. You can't afford to be off that radar.

I want to thank you for taking the time to read this book and consider the points I've discussed here. If you're looking for more information on marketing your roofing business in the digital age, I'll be more than happy to speak with you. Simply contact me at **welton@ringringmarketing.com**, or visit our website at **www.ringringmarketing.com**, or call me at **(888) 383-2848**.

Thanks again, and let me wish you and your business great success now and for many years to come.

Welton Hong

Author Contact Information

Ring Ring Marketing only makes money when our clients make money. Our work produces amazing results, so we stand behind it with a <u>60-day no-questions-asked money-back guarantee</u>.

We have a simple evaluation process for businesses interested in partnering with us. We'll discuss your particular company and how we can employ an online marketing campaign structured specifically for you.

We have had great success with all sorts of businesses, and because <u>we specialize in the roofing industry</u>, we know exactly how to design a campaign we know will be successful for you.

If the numbers don't work out and we're unable to help you, it won't cost you a penny. That's why there's <u>zero risk</u> in contacting us for an evaluation. We want to make it easy for you, because that's how the best partnerships work.

Now is the time to act. You simply can't afford to get left behind. Learn how a professionally executed Internet marketing campaign can make this your most successful year ever. Just email my office at **info@RingRingMarketing.com** or call **888-383-2848** to get started.